DAUGHTERS
OF EVE

Merry
Christmas to
a daughter of eve
from her mother
'95

DAUGHTERS OF EVE

The Magical Mysteries of Womanhood

Dolores Ashcroft-Nowicki

Aquarian/Thorsons
An Imprint of HarperCollinsPublishers

The Aquarian Press
An Imprint of HarperCollins*Publishers*
77–85 Fulham Palace Road,
Hammersmith, London W6 8JB
1160 Battery Street,
San Francisco, California 94111-1213

Published by The Aquarian Press 1993
1   3   5   7   9   10   8   6   4   2

A catalogue record for this book
is available from the British Library

ISBN 0 85030 977 8

Typeset by Harper Phototypesetters Limited,
Northampton, England
Printed in Great Britain by
Loader Jackson Printers, Bedfordshire

Contents

To my beloved spiritual sister
Anna 'Shakmah' Branche of Philadelphia

Acknowledgements

I have learned much from many women over the years, and I owe a great deal to their friendship, skill, intuition and Feminine Power. The following are but a few of those I acknowledge as being true 'Daughters of Eve'. Their names are in no particular order.

Paddy Slade, Elizabeth Anderton, Jessica Ashcroft, Tamara Ashcroft-Nowicki, Su Charles, Jackie Crabtree, Sheila Keyse, Olive Ashcroft, Margaret O'Donnell, Cassandra Carter-Lewis, Fran Keegan, Caitlín Matthews, Maureen Peters, Carrie Brennan, Lyrata, Avisan, Adanah, Azterrah, Mishanavah and the ladies of SEED, Evie Gauthier, Jane Hill, Emily Peach, Addy Kortweg, Anna van der Bogaarde, Robin LaTrobe, Mary Greer, Merlin Stone, Katherine Kurtz, Debbie Rice, Vivienne O'Regan, Naomi Ozaniec, Marian Green, Eileen Campbell, Karen Charbonneau, Ann Smith, Laurel Lander, Mary Clare Sanderson, Helene McMurtie, Dian McLellan and a lady who bore the name of Marjorie Mistlethwaite when she walked the earth and who taught me the strange and beautiful ways of The Old Tradition up in the 'North Countree'.

There are many others to whom my debt is just as great: thank you all.

Introduction

In the course of my esoteric life I have written more rituals than I care to remember, rituals of all kinds and within the discipline of many different traditions. Those offered in this book are purely for women of all ages to use and enjoy. I have covered all the major 'Rites of Passage' moments in a woman's life, as well as those occasions when a welling up of joy and sweetness from the soul explodes in a passionate worship of the Divine for no other reason than a need to integrate oneself with that awesome Divinity we know, have always known, as The Great Mother.

There have always been Mysteries and Rites that are set aside for each sex. That is the way of things: there are men and there are women; each needs the other for friendship, love, mating, although not always all of them apply to everyone. The ancient Feminine Mysteries are as valid today as they ever were, just as those for our Masculine counterparts continue to have a similar meaning for men, and we are gradually recovering others that are meant to be shared and enjoyed together in companionship rather than in rivalry. That the two polarities of the Universe, Male and Female, Positive and Negative, Form and Force, should be reflected in the separate mysteries of the Goddess and Her Horned Consort is right and proper, for then each can more fully understand their opposite.

It has been said that all things are symbolised in the glyph of the Tree of Life with its three pillars: the silver, positive pillar of the Masculine and the black, negative pillar of the Feminine, which then balance themselves in harmony within the golden middle pillar of Equilibrium. Both of the side pillars are forces in their own right for both good and bad and at various times they have been both. The Ages have come and gone and have left behind a totally changed world to that which was once hailed, rightly or wrongly, as the Golden Age.

In the latter years we have heard a great deal about the battle between Matriarchy and Patriarchy, between the Goddess and the Church, between Woman and Man. A lot of it has a sound basis, equally a lot of it has been hyped out of all recognition. But gradually a balance is appearing in the world and a harmony is seen to be emerging. Deep within the heart of every man and woman there is a longing for the withdrawn, secret, soul-deep experiences that contact with the old ways can bring. Every woman desires a re-union with her secret self, desires it, needs it, longs for it, knowing that such a union will make her whole in a way that nothing else can do. For unless a woman is fully awakened to her own personal understanding of her Womanhood, she will remain a Sleeping Beauty surrounded by the thorn bushes of her own frustrations. The same applies to every man.

There is no way back to the ancient days, to the dark caves and darker practices of Samothraki, to the wild, blood-crazed routes of the Bacchantes and the whispering groves of white-thighed Artemis through which the male victim was hunted. No longer do young girls gather to throw flowers into the sea at Paphos, hoping to see Aphrodite rise from the waves to grant their desire for a husband. But we can look back in smiling remembrance and bring forward into our own time newer, gentler versions of the ancient rites of womanhood. We can re-create the Rites of Passage from childhood through to Wise Woman. These things our modern life, with its eternal rush and noise, has stolen from us. We can use the tragically little we have saved from the past to give the modern Daughter of Eve a sense of having something that is purely hers, and for all time.

I offer this book to every woman, whatever her age, that she may have the chance to experience her true self. It will take her from birth, through all the stages of her life, to that moment when, as the Old Wise Woman, she takes her leave of the earth and passes into the womb of the Goddess, there to wait until her time comes again. Here are offered the magical mysteries of both Eve and Lillith who are really just *one* woman, for you to experience by yourself or in the company of other women. All you have to do is turn the page . . .

Dolores Ashcroft-Nowicki
Jersey, 1992

PART 1
CHILDHOOD

1

BEGINNING THE TRAINING

Children are the most prolific users of ritual. One only has to watch them in a playground using time-honoured methods of choosing sides, or chanting the old rhymes used in the same way for hundreds of years to see the truth of this. For the most part children follow the herd instinct when very young and copy their peers in mannerisms, usage of words and games, and some quite strange and even ancient beliefs and habits. (There are, of course, always exceptions, and some solitary children show highly-developed psychic tendencies that may or may not persist after puberty.) Ritual comes easily to them and unlike adults they have not yet had time to build a barrier against belief in the unseen.

By the age of four or five most children are able to join in a celebration and both enjoy the occasion and understand its basic meaning. There is no need to overburden them with long-winded explanations; a simple outline is enough. Little girls will enjoy the idea of dressing up in a simple white dress and wearing ribbon crowns in the Spring, gathering flowers and binding them into long ropes to dance with in the Summer, or helping to glean for corn in the Harvest fields and learning to make corn dollies as their great grandmothers did. When Winter comes it is time for the celebration of the return of the Sun Child and the excitement of watching for the first star to appear.

The learning of basic herbal lore will stand children of both sexes in good stead, and the ancient ways of Albion will sink deep into their memories to be passed on to the next generation in their turn. Teaching the art of meditation to children is giving them a means to combat stress and its dangers from an early age. Children as young as three and four and even younger can suffer from extreme stress. Adults try to keep up 'with the Joneses', or worry about their jobs, children try to keep up with their peer group, suffer persecution in classroom and playground alike, and in severe cases can suffer complete breakdowns or even attempt, and sometimes succeed in, actually committing suicide.

Far from harming them or filling their heads with nonsense, simple rituals encourage children to form a bond with the earth and its creatures. If this bond does not come into existence the child grows up unknowing and uncaring of the adult role of Caretaker to our Planet Earth.

Between the ages of four and eight all children are at their most impressionable. From then on up to the age of twelve they are still open to change but slightly less so. By the time they start school the way they will view adult life and its problems will already be set. Changing those ideas in later life will be hard, will take a long time, and will almost certainly cause a fair amount of trauma. It is an area where teachers and parents must, if the child is to grow physically, mentally and spiritually, work closely together.

Patterns of behaviour and social manners, the way a child approaches problems and bonds with its peer group are learned at home. It is not a teacher's place to show a child how to behave in public, but that of the parents, though the teacher can certainly help matters with continued encouragement. Equally, a parent may leave the task of teaching a child how to learn, to gather, process and correlate data, to the teacher, but can help enormously by working with the teacher in an atmosphere of cooperation. They may also help by seeing that homework is done and by upholding school disciplines. All too often teachers and parents seem to be on opposite sides of the fence, and when this happens the real loser is the child.

By the same token, a child can learn from both parents and teachers to care for the environment and the other species that share the earth with us. Magical play along with carefully selected meditations, pathworkings and rituals can stimulate such attitudes from an early age. The child will then grow into a responsible adult without the need to change ideas, principles and ingrained habits that are detrimental to the world around them.

Pathworkings offer a child a means to expand that most vital of senses, the imagination. It teaches them to visualise, or really 'see' the objects and landscapes around them. It can help them to assimilate and memorise, to train their recall abilities which in turn will help their school work. All these things are part and parcel of much older techniques once known to those who studied and trained in the ancient Mysteries. Many of these training methods are still used today in ordinary ways. Sportsmen and women use the technique of pathworking and inner visualisation to sharpen their game or sports discipline. Dancers, housewives, policemen, doctors and MPs use meditation as a means of relieving stress. If taught in childhood, such talents become part of the adult life and are never lost. Such practices should be taught in schools as a part of the curriculum, encouraging every child to spend a few minutes each day seeking the inner silence that gives peace, serenity and confidence.

Rituals for very young children are best kept short with alternating sequences of quietness and action. This means their attention span can be gradually lengthened and made stronger over a period of time, and in turn this will enhance their learning power in school. Care must be taken to ensure that the children do not place too much emphasis on the deeper areas of the work until they are old enough to understand the need to use 'Discretion and Discrimination', the traditional watchwords of all practitioners of the Mysteries. The rites written for this age group are meant for small groups of girls with a few adult women mixed in, for guidance and safety. None of them are long or over demanding.

What may safely be taught to a child between the ages of four and twelve without overburdening them? Firstly, the ability to sit still. This sounds silly, but it is something children find hard to do, to the despair of their teachers. The average time for a child's (4–8 years) span of complete attention is approximately five minutes. (There are occasions when they are totally caught up in the wonder of some object or event and they can become absorbed for much longer.) After that their attention wanders, even if briefly. With gentle training this period can be increased to ten minutes. The ability to concentrate is seldom actually *taught* to children, but we expect them to do it nevertheless. 'Pay attention' is a remark that is engraved on the youthful psyche of every adult. If taught via the ancient techniques it is a skill that can become part of their life.

Responsibility comes with growth, but the basics can be taught from early on, and we are talking here about both sexes, not simply the feminine. Without the ability to sit quietly and still, and to concentrate on a given focal point, not even an adult can work magic or a ritual. Like it or not, and certain factions do not like it at all, the quality of inner stillness is essential to mental health in this modern world. Those of us who practise the old ways, whether it be the Craft, or neo-Paganism or the Western Mystery Tradition, have the fundamental right to raise our children in our own traditions. The United Nations Charter gives us this right, therefore let us exercise it, and let no one take it away from us.

We all tend to underestimate the ability of a child to understand things. They may not be able to verbalise that understanding but in most cases it is there. Children's television is one of the worst offenders in this way, by entertaining at the expense of the child's intelligence, and yet it can also come up with things that are so right it is truly magical, for instance well-presented fairy tales, and series such as *The Box of Delights* and *The Moon Dial* for older children. I have seen children walk away from the screen, switch it off, or turn to a toy or book when a particularly asinine afternoon programme is offered to them. The presenters mostly adopt the traditional smile that reaches just to the top lip, and the saccharine tone of voice that immediately tells a bright child that it is being talked down to. When you feel tempted to use such a tone to a child, remember that the child in question can set the timer on your video machine and it is likely that you can't! They had to *invent* a special gadget to enable adults to do that!

To teach a child to sit still and be quiet needs patience, but it can be done. First you must catch the child's attention: there must be a good reason for it to be still. Start with two minutes and work up to five over ten days or so. Keep to five minutes for about a week, then gently add another minute once every three or four days until they can sit still and quiet for up to eight minutes. From eight years old they can train themselves to work up to ten or even twelve minutes.

You can cover two techniques together by teaching them to visualise at the same time. Give them an oven timer set for two minutes and sit with them while it ticks off the seconds to show them how long two minutes can be. Then, having reset the timer, give them a picture to look at and to remember. It should be a picture they like, maybe a favourite one from a story book. Tell them to look at it for two minutes without speaking, just looking, and remembering everything they can see. For a few days you will probably have to sit with them, let them know you are there and working with them. This helps them to understand that while they can consider this to be a game, it is an important game.

When the time is up ask them questions about the picture and give them a small prize, say one Smartie or chocolate button for every two right answers. Once a day is enough for a young child. It must never cease to be a game between you. When you are out together you might draw a child's attention to a window display, or an advertising hoarding. Ask them to look at it while you to count to sixty, then continue walking and ask them questions about it. In such ways you will not only teach your small Daughter of Eve the value and relaxation of sitting quiet and still, but you will be training her ability to visualise and to observe the world around her.

Ask them to count how many people are wearing something red when you are out for a walk. How many different kinds of cars, how many little girls with plaits, etc. You can use a modified version of 'Kim's Game' a form of training that is used in adult observation tests. Use a medium-sized tray and some coloured marbles or even Smarties. Use different numbers of each colour. Allow the child to look for sixty seconds, then cover the tray. Ask how many blue, how many red, green, etc. Then ask what corner the blues were in, what colour was the centre group. What colour was the largest group. Allow them to have one group of the sweets as a prize.

This teaches them to concentrate, to observe intently, and it also trains their short-term memory. They are playing games certainly, but games that are training and fine-tuning their minds. Another way of teaching them to be quiet and still and which prepares them for both pathworkings and meditation, is inner imagery. Go back to the favourite fairy tale and ask them to choose a character. Then ask them to close their eyes and describe that character to you.

Once they can be still for at least five minutes you can begin to train them to meditate. Give them a colour and ask them to think about the colour, how it feels, how it makes them feel when they are wearing it. What kind of flower is that colour, and if it had a taste or a smell, can they imagine what it would be like. Tell them to think about all this and at the end of five minutes to come and tell you what they have found out.

Ask them to think about being on the beach, or in the swimming pool, and to imagine swimming from one end to the other. Get them to concentrate on each stroke as they make it in the mind. When they can do this, give them a flower, or a photograph of someone they love to look at and meditate (think) about. At this age it is more like contemplation than real meditation, but it is a beginning and the ability will grow.

Give them a list of flowers, herbs and fruits for each season, and ask them to learn it by heart. Explain why we have Holly and Mistletoe in Winter and what they mean. Tell them what flowers are the first to greet the Spring Queen, and which are the flowers the Summer Lady wears in her hair. There are many stories about the various Corn Dollies that can be used to elaborate in Harvest Time and Autumn. The older and more adult themes that are the heritage of all Daughters of Eve can be left until they can fully understand them.

Children who are not taught ritual will sometimes devise them for their own use. They also obey an inner wellspring of arcane knowledge in their playground games. There is a rhythmic and seasonal aspect to children's games that is seldom noticed by adults. There is a time and a season for skipping ropes and for other rope games, another for hop-scotch and for ring games. Marbles and line games such as Oranges and Lemons also have their inner phases, coming and going in accordance to some long established lore of childhood. Children are creatures of ritual and understand it on a purer level than many who would call themselves adepts.

Children need also to deal with death as an everyday occurrence. They need to bury their pets and mourn them. When the time comes it is then easier to lose the older members of the family, close relatives or even school friends.

They need to know how to cope with loss and the best way is through ritual.

Each season of our lives contains what we call Rites of Passage. They are the times when we learn through an event, an experience, a sorrow or a joy, when we grow through that passing and leave a little of ourselves behind, and add a new piece to use in the future that lies ahead of us. For children of four to twelve we might single out the following events:

1 The first day of real school
2 The first time in hospital or away from home
3 The death of a friend or relative, or of a loved pet
4 The annual birthday
5 New home or new school

Of course these rituals may be altered to suit boys as well as girls, but because of the nature of this book, and its title, they are written primarily for girls. Maybe in time I will get around to writing *Sons of Adam* for little boys . . . of all ages.

One of the things that children must be taught from the start is the practice of keeping silence. It must be made clear from the very beginning that these little rituals are experiences which cannot be shared with school friends no matter how dear or how close. This is for their own protection and for yours. The other and most important teaching is that they must be taught to accord respect to all traditions, to acknowledge the Creative Deity in the name by which both they and others may call that ONE.

If we are to build a world without prejudice and religious bigotry then we must teach our children *now*. The future lies with them, not us, so they must begin to build the bridges between faiths. We live in an era when the old ways are breaking down and new ways are beginning to form. All the barriers are coming down, waves of emigrants are moving across the world in a long slow wave. Nothing like it has been seen since the Celts left their birthplace in the Indus valley and began their millennia-long trek to the West. Before this age ends our descendants will have crossed the barrier of space and will have come face to face with stranger life forms and Faiths than we could ever imagine. Now is the time to prepare for that future.

2

MEDITATIONS AND PATHWORKINGS

With young children up to the age of eight or nine it is often best to meditate together as a family group. This gives the child a feeling of support and encouragement, especially when the idea of meditating is very new. Once the habit is ingrained it will grow with the child and open up new vistas in every aspect of their lives. The slower child will find a release from the stress of feeling inadequate against a quicker peer group. This is particularly so with a dyslexic child. The bright child will find it gives a depth to the thinking process that will prove of great value in school work and at home or in outside activities.

As parents we might think towards a time when meditation can be taught in schools by teachers qualified to do so. Until that time the burden lies on us, the mothers, and fathers too, to encourage our children in a practice that can only be of benefit to them throughout their lives.

The first thing to instil is the discipline needed to meditate at the same time every second day, or until the child is ready to make it a daily occurrence. Some children will not want to do it and should be gently coaxed into trying it for a few minutes. Others will come to it naturally. Talk to them about the Centring process, tell them of the special inner place where they can rest, be at peace, feel secure and safe. Help them to build such a place through visualisation. It might be a fairytale cottage in a wood; a forest clearing filled with friendly trees and animals; a seashore where mermaids sing and dolphins swim, or a treetop house. You will find other ideas and seed sentences will come to you when you begin to work with them. It is a good idea to write down anything you may read or hear and keep it for future use.

Remember also that a meditation can be done while walking. You might decide upon a subject or simply a sound they can repeat either silently or in an undertone as they walk. This is more difficult as their attention is inclined to wander more often, but it is an alternative for hyperactive children who can find it very difficult to relax enough to sit and meditate in the usual way.

To teach young children how to centre themselves, you nearly always have to rely on an image to which they can relate. To an adult we say '. . . go inwards and downwards'. To a child it is better to say, '. . . let's go exploring the inside of our heads. Hold my hand and close your eyes and we will pretend we are going down in a lift. Can you imagine the way your tummy feels when the lift stops? Your tummy is always a little bit late in catching up. When the door opens we can see the entrance to a big cave with a clean sandy floor and lots of little crystals in the walls. Fixed to the walls are torches, just like the ones they had in castles a long time ago. Let's go and explore and see what we can find.

'We will walk into the cave and keep on walking. The way slopes down and turns in a spiral to the right. As we walk the way gets a little narrower and a little darker, but because the cave is inside your own head you can't really get lost. Now we come to the really narrow part and it's going to get very dark. But I'm still holding your hand. Suddenly we come to the end of the tunnel. There is a big mirror standing against the wall and it is a magic mirror and shines with a light all of its own. Look into it and think hard and it will show you anything you want to see.'

At this point you can introduce the symbol, sentence, image or object of the meditation. A nervous child can be allowed torches all the way, but encouraged to gradually reduce their number until fear of the dark is overcome. You can bring them back the same way. Alternatives can be used: climbing a stairway into a turret tower; jumping into a rabbit hole like Alice in Wonderland and drifting down like a feather, and returning through a small door leading to the everyday world.

Do not be afraid to use traditional symbols. They have a way of explaining themselves and opening up to an exploring mind. Children have less 'wrong programming' of which to rid themselves than adults, and given a chance will take to this kind of thing like a duck to water.

Pathworking for children can be a total joy. They already have all that is needed: a rich imagination and the natural ability to use and enjoy it. They can be used in many ways: to relax them before sleep, especially when over excited or needing to rest; to keep them quiet and still during an illness or after surgery or an accident; to help them with school work, and also purely for recreation.

Pathworkings should be kept fairly short even for older children, and they must always be taught that they are not to overindulge in them. Those being used to increase knowledge and understanding should be supervised until a child is about ten, by which time they will have enough experience to use them wisely.

They are particularly good for use with sport and PE problems. Children can also be taught to heal themselves from injury or illness. It can keep them amused, quiet and resting on long journeys, and they can do interactive workings in a small group without too much, or even any, adult supervision. As they get older they will find other uses for such workings of their own accord.

Young children are very close to the inner world, they are fresh and new to the physical level and can still glimpse the higher levels. However, each day takes them further away and into the earthly life destined for them. This is why it is so important that they are taught to appreciate and use their inner powers and talents while the spiritual bloom is still upon their souls. In the orthodox religions they are introduced early to the church, its teachings and its ceremonies, as indeed are the children of recognised religions such as Islam, Hinduism and Buddhism. Surely we can do no less for those children born and raised in the minority faiths.

If ritual and meditation are to be an on-going part of a child's life then it is as well to make them a robe. Cotton, linen or polyester are advised, as they are easily washable and can be bought in a variety of shades. For a young girl white or cream is really the best, but she may express a wish to have a favourite colour. In this case go by the child's need rather than by what you, as an adult, think is best. It should be quite plain with a round neck and slightly wider than usual sleeves.

Perhaps some bands of colour around the hem, or a cord of some bright and cheerful colour.

This is not to be confused with the traditional white dress of the little May Queen which is more of a party dress with a full skirt and fancy sleeves and a sash. Ballet slippers are best for their feet. Choose the fabric ones rather than leather which soon wear through and are expensive to buy. A small amulet or a pretty necklace of coral or amber, to be kept for special occasions, can be added. It is a nice idea to give such a necklace as a birthday or Christmas gift.

The following ideas for meditation are graded for ages four to six, and seven to ten.

Meditations

Four to Six

1 *The House* Draw a picture of a house, or ask the child to draw it, but do not colour it in any way. Just make it an ordinary house with a door and windows. Ask the child to look at the drawing while you count to fifty out loud. Then both close your eyes, build the image internally and think about the house. Keep looking at the image inside your head, think of nothing but the house and keep on thinking about it. Ask yourself what a house does, what materials are used to build it. Think of the rooms, how many and what kind, and how they are decorated. After three minutes, you should both open your eyes and allow a few minutes for orientation. Then ask the child to talk about her thoughts. It helps if you write them down, or if the child is capable of doing this it is a good thing to instil the idea of keeping records from the beginning.

2 *The Cat* Show the child a picture of a cat or a kitten and again allow some fifty or sixty seconds' viewing time. Then ask her to close her eyes and think about the picture. This time you can ask her questions as a way of getting her to concentrate on the object. Is the cat full grown or a kitten? How many legs does a cat have? Does it have whiskers? How are a cat's eyes different to ours? What kind of things does a cat eat? How do they climb trees so quickly?

This kind of questioning keeps the image in the child's mind and keeps her looking at it in a concentrated way.

3 *The Ball* Give the child a ball, or a picture of a ball to look at. Allow fifty to sixty seconds for imprinting the image, then ask the child to close her eyes and just think about the ball. Think about it bouncing along the pavement, or off a wall, floating in the sea, or just lying on the ground waiting to be picked up. You can help initially by recording the word BALL on a tape, repeating it every five seconds. This helps to keep the young mind on the subject. Again, ask questions afterwards and keep a record of both questions and answers.

For children this young it is best to keep to simple everyday subjects that the child knows well. Always allow about one minute for viewing and then two to three minutes of meditation time. From here you can go on to more abstract things. In the summer you can ask her to lie on the grass and look up at the clouds and just watch them change shape. Give her a small flower, like a daisy or a buttercup and ask her simply to look at it and think about it for a whole minute. Small and simple as this exercise seems, it can lay the foundation for the ability to concentrate at a later date when she begins school. For older children, those of seven to ten, the subjects and the length of time can be made just that much harder and longer.

Seven to Ten

At this age the child can be taught to sit either cross-legged on a cushion on the floor or in a chair with a firm back and cushions under her feet to support them and her legs in an approximation of the adult 'Godform' position. Care must be taken not to impose undue strain on the young back.

1 *The Horse* Talk about the horse as an animal of transportation, both pulling carts and being ridden. Discuss the types of horse, perhaps pointing them out in a book: the Arab, the Shire, the Quarter Horse, the Palomino, etc. Give the child a handful of very small stones or buttons. Then ask her to close her eyes and bring up the image of a horse in her mind, and keep that image as long as she can without losing it or thinking about other things.

Every time she finds herself thinking about something different she is to place a stone or a button on the floor in front of her, or into a bowl in her lap or on a table next to her, but with as little disruption as possible to the meditation. Count how many times the attention has wandered after each session and encourage the child to aim for as little distraction of attention as possible. This kind of self check may be applied to all the meditation subjects in this age group and the next.

2 *A Seedling in a Pot* The seedling should be well above the earth and easily seen. Show the child a picture of the mature plant/flower and ask her to meditate on the gradual growth of the plant, seeing it at each stage right up to the flowering. This can be stretched over several days with a meditation on the final day including a full look at the plant from its root system to the bloom.

3 *A Green Triangle* Now we are getting into a more abstract frame of mind. Ask the child to draw and colour a large triangle and look at it for a few minutes. Encourage her to look away at a piece of plain card and take note of the projected image in its complimentary colour. Explain that this will be harder to 'hold onto' but that she should try her best. At this age a child can well distinguish between active and passive meditation, if it is explained that during active work one should think hard about the subject and see how many things one can find out about it simply by thinking about it and looking at it inside one's head. Passive meditation is just letting thoughts drift in and out of one's head, but always keeping them tuned to the subject and not allowing stray thoughts to interfere.

Different subjects might include simple symbolic shapes such as a five-pointed Star, The Green Man, or a Wheatsheaf. You might also use seasonal and traditional symbols such as the Easter Hare, Santa Claus, or any of the delightful illustrations from the Flower Fairy books. Fairytale characters can also be used, as well as everyday objects around the house or the surrounding countryside. Once the child is used to the idea of going inward it is time to begin teaching her to meditate upon her name, and then her mirror image, and finally herself from the inside. Children can understand far more than we imagine, and given the right kind of encouragement they will respond well to the joy of inner discoveries.

Pathworkings

Four to Six

Bedtime pathworkings serve several purposes for younger children. It allows them to use and strengthen their creativity and imagination. It encourages them to keep a regular bedtime. But perhaps most important of all it helps them to sleep and lessens the possibility of nightmares and disturbed sleep patterns. However, they must be chosen or 'built' with care, with no overstimulating scenarios and no monsters, trolls, or characters that might frighten or confuse them.

Having said that I am all for creating a Guardian who is always introduced into bedtime pathworkings with the express purpose of keeping nightmares, etc, at bay. This Guardian should be large enough to give the child confidence in it, fearsome enough to deter danger, and yet have an endearing quality or flaw that enables the child to be top dog at times. For instance, a comfortable-sized dragon of a distinctly cuddly appearance, perhaps pastel coloured. If female it could wear a large apron and a lace mop cap and have long eyelashes and an addiction to Earl Grey Tea. It might also be afraid of mice or have a tendency to nibble its claws when agitated. If male it might wear fancy waistcoats (vests to our American readers) and a bow tie, and have holes in its socks. Nice and Disney-esque, but at the slightest sign of danger to the child the Guardian becomes a fire-breathing protector quite capable of seeing off anything even remotely harmful. The illustrations will show exactly what I mean.

Other protectors might be Unicorns, Bears, Wooden Soldiers, Hippos, or a giant-sized Postman Pat. A policeman might be a good idea and can help the child to relate to the real thing instead of, as is so often the case, being warned that policemen are there to punish naughty children.

To establish a Guardian, first show the child the picture, or a picture of the protector required. Ask them if they would like it to be a 'Mother' type Guardian or a 'Father/Uncle' type.

Practise building up the figure together, decide where it will live when not needed. A small box, an old bottle, a paper house the child can build herself; anything of this nature will do. The Guardian can emerge when needed or called on in the form of coloured smoke like a Genie (in fact a Genie makes a very good protector), or even be held in something the child carries with her all the time, like a little locket, a ring, or a tiny pill box she can carry in her pocket. When the child can picture her new friend quite clearly in her head it is time for the next step, the naming and the all-important 'Call'.

Names in magical circles are of the utmost importance. It would not be too much to say that the whole power of the Guardian lies in its name. I would suggest therefore that this name be something that only the child and her mother should know and keep secret. It should also be a name not likely to be guessed by others. When speaking of it in front of others it might be referred to by a totally different name. A short but

effective naming ceremony of the Guardian might be
something like this.

The mother or older sister, or whoever is the other holder
of the true name, holds the picture of the chosen protector.
The child writes that name with a finger dipped in water on
the back of the picture. Then she writes it in the earth with
a stick and sprinkles fresh earth over it to hide it. It is written
for the third time in the air with an incense stick, and finally
in fire using a lighted taper to trace the name over hot
charcoal. Thus the name is written in Earth, Water, Fire and
Air. The Call is fixed in the same way, but spoken out loud
as the writing is completed.

Now a short pathworking must be built to call forth the
Guardian. It should contain a brief visualisation of the
protector issuing from its container and taking up a selected
spot in the room, beside the bed, by the door or window or
in front of a cupboard the child might think of as hiding a
bedtime 'nasty'. The trigger is the Call which is pronounced

three times, and then the name followed by a greeting between the Guardian and the child. It is enjoined to keep watch over the child through the night both when waking and asleep, and to return to its place just before its charge wakes up in the morning. A blessing on the protector should also be included. Of course the Guardian can also be taken into the bedtime pathworking if it is desired as a companion as well as a protector.

It is important that the Guardian is called up every night before the bedtime pathworking so it can enter the working with the child if she wishes. It can be given a specific task such as looking under beds, and into dark cupboards and corners that a young child may find frightening. Evening workings are best when they are of the type that can carry the child over into sleep. A magic carpet on which they can climb and look over the edge at the landscape as they fly is always enjoyed. Turning the bed itself into some kind of vehicle, such as a coach drawn by Cloud Horses, makes the child feel safe and snug. Help the child to visualise the ground below and any landmarks. If, as an adult, you can remember the sheer magic of the journey over a moonlit London Town in Disney's *Peter Pan* then this is what to aim for in your narration.

The Guardian itself can become part of this as follows. Let us imagine that we have called out your child's Guardian, a large purple dragonette that she has named Harriet:

She is standing beside your bed and polishing her scales with a scented hanky and making sure that her lace cap is on straight. She wears a knitted shawl around her shoulders and has on a clean white apron with a very big pocket in the front. Close your eyes and imagine that you are becoming much smaller then you really are and when you are small enough, Harriet picks you up in her claws, very gently, places you in her pocket and fastens you in with a big safety pin. It is just deep enough so you can look out safely, but not fall out.

Harriet waddles over to the window and opens it wide, and because she is a magic dragonette she can make it even wider so she can squeeze through. Very few people know that Harriet has the most beautiful purple wings, because she keeps them neatly folded away under her shawl. She take off her shawl and folds it up, putting it on the bottom of your bed. Harriet is a very tidy dragonette indeed. Then she squeezes through the window, sits on the ledge for a minute to get her breath and then . . . she jumps! As she jumps she spreads her wings, the wind catches them and you find yourself flying up and up, higher and higher until the houses are just tiny boxes far below. Can you lean out and look down at them?

Harriet is flying towards the sea, her wings are very strong and beat the air in long steady strokes. You are nice and warm in her pocket because dragons have a lot of fire inside them and her warmth comes right through her apron. Now you can see the ocean and the big ships sailing from one country to another. Harriet flies lower and very close, close enough for you to see people in the big dining room eating their dinner and dancing to an orchestra. Of course they can't see Harriet or you because you are wrapped around with magic to keep you safe.

On and on you fly until your eyes get tired with looking and seeing all these strange and wonderful things. Tall mountains with snow caps, great icebergs floating in the northern seas, huge forests that seem to go on forever, and little islands with long golden beaches. As you go Harriet tells you tales about her life when she was very young. Dragons live for hundreds of years so she can tell you about things she saw when your great-great-grandmother was a little girl. But now you are very tired and you curl up in the bottom of Harriet's pocket and let yourself swing to and fro as she turns to fly back home. You will not remember flying through the window or Harriet tucking you into bed. Then she sits down beside the bed and gets out her knitting and watches over you until morning. Good night Harriet, thank you and bless you for keeping us safe.

Seven to Ten

The Island of Dreams
Begin by looking through an atlas. Look at the islands scattered over the planet, look at their size and shape and read about their types of climate. See what grows in the way of fruit and other things to eat. What about the geography of these islands, do they have mountains or just hills, have they got rivers or just streams. What kind of animals live on them?

When you have learned as much as you can, take a piece of plain paper and some coloured pencils and draw the shape of an island, not one you have seen, but *your* island as you would like it to be. Don't make it too big, but big enough for it to have several different kinds of places. It might have several long sandy beaches and one deep inlet that could serve as a harbour for a ship. The centre might be a small mountain high enough to have snow on the top and a river wide enough to need a bridge. Add several small streams, and perhaps a small forest. Think about what kind of fruit trees you would like and what kind of animals and birds.

Colour in the areas of trees and mark the place where you would like to live. It might be a warm dry cave, or a tree house high in the branches. It might be one made from palm leaves and branches on the seashore. Make it as detailed as you can. When you have done this decide what kind of climate it will have, and what kind of weather. Remember, a tropical island may have tornadoes and hurricanes.

Now make a list of things you think you will need. Things like matches, an axe and a whetstone with which to keep it sharp. A hunting knife to cut branches and leaves, a compass and a magnifying glass. A large plastic can to hold water, a length of rope, a calendar or a diary and a pencil. A large tarpaulin might be useful and a sewing kit. Lastly, a length of twine and some fish hooks. In addition to these things you may take six more articles with you of your own choice.

Now you are ready to make your first journey. Make yourself comfortable and close your eyes. Think about the island until you can see it behind your eyelids. Make it as real as you can until you can smell the sea and hear the wind, and feel it on your face. Wriggle your toes and feel the sand on your bare feet, or paddle in the sea. Take your time, you do not have to find out everything about your island on the first visit. Have you thought of a name for your island? Well you should. Think of the names some islands have been given in fiction. Lilliput, Hispaniola, Melindi, and so on. One thing you should know about this island, it changes from time to time. It may get bigger or smaller, it may surprise you with a hill or cave or wood that you have never seen before.

The other thing about the island is that there is nothing really dangerous on it, no poisonous snakes or spiders, only the friendly kind that may or may not talk to you . . . as most of the animals and occasional trees may well do.

There are no monsters although if you have a nasty temper or you are not very nice inside, you may come up against that side of yourself and have to deal with it. Neither can you change the weather – it will rain, shine, thunder, get hot and cold according to the general inconsistency of weather in the real world. (Maybe one of your extras should be a large umbrella.)

Your first need will be shelter, and according to your choice it will be waiting for you . . . however, you have to find it and it might be anywhere. You may not even find it the first time on the island. You see, because it is *your* very own island it will always appear how you want it to appear, dull and gloomy or full of sunshine according to your mood when you get there.

All the heavy things ordered for you can be found in the shelter, the smaller things are in a backpack at your feet. One more thing – listen, do you hear that bark? Look just coming out of the trees is a dog, and it has been waiting for you to come. While you are in the real world it will guard your island and will be here to welcome you when you come. It has plenty of water and it will catch food for itself, but it will be able to show you around. It *may* speak to you from time to time, but mostly it will keep its silence. Its name is LOB. This is a very old alternative English name for Puck, a Hobgoblin who has a friendly relationship with humans.

So, this is your very own island in which you can have many wonderful adventures, it is up to you what you do and how you do it. Just remember that most of the same rules apply as in the real world. You will have to learn how to cope with things like wet matches, how to clean fish, and how to put worms on hooks. You must teach yourself to light a fire safely and how to prevent it from spreading into the woods. If your matches run out you have the glass, you can start a fire with that. How? Well that is something you can find out in the real world by asking questions.

One last warning: this can be a lot of fun, but also hard work and very addictive, so you must not allow yourself to go there too often, once or twice a week is enough. Just before going to sleep is a good time as you can often take the whole thing over into dreams.

There are as yet very few books offering meditation subjects and pathworkings for children. This is a state of affairs I hope to rectify in the near future. For those willing to write their own, my book *Highways of the Mind* will offer some help.

3

THE RITUALS

Rituals are used for many reasons: for protection; for healing; for guidance or for the celebration of specific moments in our lives. There are of course other reasons, but they can be learned gradually. Between the ages of four and twelve there are several occasions that might considered minor Rites of Passage in the life of a young Daughter of Eve. I have thought over my choice very carefully and consulted other women – teachers, mothers and grandparents among them – for their views, but inevitably I have been curtailed by space. I have kept all the rites as short and simple as possible, but as the child grows older they can of course be extended.

My final selection is as follows:

1 The first day of school (not nursery school)
2 Hospitalisation
3 The first time away from home and parents
4 Death a) pet, b) friend, c) grandparent d) parent

Items 2 and 3 run parallel with one another as the first time away from home is often for medical reasons. However, I took into consideration reasons such as boarding school, Summer Camps, and the increasing tendency for school classes to go on holiday together. At first glance it might be thought that all the choices seem a little gloomy. While this is true it must be realised that for the most part it is at such times that the child grows in wisdom and experience. All are, in point of fact, bone fide 'Passage Rites'. In each case the child passes through an experience; some will be a genuine First Time, but there will be others that may be repeated, like birthdays. But in every case the child will leave something of herself behind and gain a new part during the passage itself.

All rituals need an opening and a closing sequence and this can be the same for any number of different rituals. For young children the simpler they are the better, but it must be vivid enough to be imprinted on their memory and on their subconscious. I have therefore devised an opening and a closing that can be utilised for them all. The Guardian appears in all of the rituals by right of that special relationship the child will have built with it. By now this is the strength of such a Being, in that it acts not only as a protector, but also as a friend, confidant, adviser, and comforter.

Opening and Closing
Until such time as the child can do this for herself an adult may do it for/with her. Stand facing east if the direction is known, if not then face any direction. The Inner Levels *have* no direction and that is where the ritual is ultimately worked.

Close your eyes and think of a large, friendly smiling sun peeping over a hill. Feel the warmth on your face and say (in your head *if not alone*):

THE SUN IN THE EAST MEANS LIGHT AND LIFE.
Make a quarter turn to the right, and think of a large, friendly dog and say:
THE DOG IN THE SOUTH MEANS PROTECTION AND SAFETY. (The Guardian can be used instead of the dog if need be.)
Make a quarter turn again, think of a silver star over the sea and say:
THE STAR IN THE WEST MEANS A SAFE PASSAGE HOME.
Make a quarter turn again and think of a table with a loaf of fresh bread and a glass of milk and say:
BREAD AND MILK IN THE NORTH MEANS COMFORT AND LOVE.
Turn back to the East again and say:
THERE IS LIGHT AROUND ME AND LIGHT WITHIN ME. I AM SAFE FROM HARM.
Simple as it is this is enough to cast a circle of protection and cleansing.

The closing sequence is just as simple. Face the North and

think of the bread with a slice half eaten and the glass half
empty and say:
I AM LOVED AND COMFORTED.
Make a quarter turn to the left, think of the Star over the
sea and say:
I AM ON MY WAY HOME.
Make a quarter turn to the left again, think of the Dog or
Guardian and say:
I AM SAFE AND PROTECTED.
Make another quarter turn and think of the sun, but this
time setting behind the hill and say:
I AM FULL OF LIGHT AND LIFE.
Stand still for a minute then say:
THERE IS LIGHT AROUND ME AND LIGHT WITHIN
ME. I AM SAFE FROM HARM.

This all that is needed for the rituals in this section and in Part
2. In fact they can be used for any age group and will prove
as effective as any of the more elaborate openings and closings
given in magical text books (including my own!). Now for the
Passage Rite.

The First Day of School

Many modern children have little or no fear of school; neither
of mine showed the slightest worry, beyond the indignity of
being kissed by their mother at the gate. For others it is a
traumatic time that heralds the end of *pure* childhood, free of
scholastic restraints. From now on they will become part of
another group mind, that of their school and their peer group.
They will come into contact with jealousies, bullying, and the
unaccountable likes and dislikes that are part of school life.
Their educational programming will begin. The Sunday
before will be a memorable one and they can understand that
they are passing from one part of their life to another. Let them
choose what they want to do: a visit to the zoo, or the cinema,
or an outing of some kind. After tea the 'Passing Through
Ceremony' can begin.

Opening and Call to the Guardian

1st Adult: (Guardian's name), YOU ARE SUMMONED HERE TODAY AS (child's name) BEGINS HER FIRST RITE OF PASSAGE. TOMORROW SHE BECOMES A SCHOOLGIRL AND BEGINS A NEW TIME IN HER LIFE. YOUR PART IN THAT NEW LIFE MUST NOW INCLUDE KEEPING HER SAFE IN SCHOOL AND OUTSIDE OF IT. YOU MUST PROTECT HER DURING THE DAY AS WELL AS AT NIGHT. DO YOU UNDERSTAND HOW IMPORTANT THIS IS?

Wait for a few moments to allow for the information to reach the thoughtform. Do not make any mistakes about this, the Guardian is as real in its dimension as you are in yours.

2nd Adult: STEP FORWARD. (Child comes forward.) ON (day) THE (date) OF (month) YOU, (child's name), WILL GO THROUGH THE FIRST RITE OF PASSAGE AND BEGIN YOUR EDUCATION. THIS IS A VERY SOLEMN MOMENT FOR US ALL, WE ARE VERY PROUD OF YOU AND TOMORROW, WHEN YOU GO INTO YOUR CLASSROOM FOR THE FIRST TIME, YOU WILL FACE MANY NEW THINGS IN YOUR LIFE. YOU WILL HAVE TO LEARN TO WORK WITH OTHERS AND TO TRY TO UNDERSTAND THEM. YOU WILL FIND SOME ARE NICE AND SOME ARE NOT, SOME WHO ARE FRIENDLY AND OTHERS WHO DO NOT LIKE YOU. THIS IS PART OF GROWING UP AND IT WILL NOT BE EASY. BUT, YOU WILL HAVE YOUR GUARDIAN, AND YOU WILL HAVE MUMMY AND DADDY (adjust if needed) AT HOME. YOU MUST LEARN TO BE BRAVE, TRUTHFUL, GENTLE, STRONG WHEN IT IS NEEDED, HELPFUL TO OTHERS, CLEAN AND TIDY. ARE YOU WILLING TO TRY?

Child: I, (name), PROMISE THAT I WILL TRY TO BE BRAVE, TRUTHFUL, GENTLE, AND STRONG. I WILL TRY TO BE HELPFUL TO OTHERS, CLEAN AND TIDY AND TO MAKE YOU AND THE TEACHERS PROUD OF ME.

1st Adult: TO HELP YOU TO REMEMBER THIS DAY WE HAVE SOMETHING TO GIVE YOU. (This gift may be something like a locket and chain, a lucky silver charm that can be pinned securely into a coat pocket, or simply a pencil box, it is a token of the Moment.) REMEMBER AS YOU GO THROUGH SCHOOL THAT YOU WILL HAVE TIMES

WHEN YOU ARE SAD OR LONELY OR ANGRY, MAYBE ALL OF THEM. BUT REMEMBER ALSO THAT NOTHING LASTS FOREVER AND THAT YOU WILL GET THROUGH TO THE OTHER SIDE OF YOUR FEELINGS. AS YOU GROW BIGGER YOU WILL UNDERSTAND MORE, AND MORE WILL BE EXPECTED OF YOU. MAKE A SPACE EACH DAY TO BE BY YOURSELF AND TO THINK OVER WHAT THAT DAY HAS BROUGHT. NEVER BE AFRAID TO SAY YOU WERE WRONG, OR THAT YOU ARE SORRY. BY THE SAME TOKEN DO NOT BE AFRAID TO STAND UP FOR YOURSELF. FROM THIS MOMENT YOU HAVE PASSED THROUGH YOUR FIRST RITE OF PASSAGE AND WE ACKNOWLEDGE YOU AS A SCHOOLGIRL, A BABY NO LONGER, BUT SOMEONE WITH A FULL SAY IN FAMILY LIFE.

Child: THANK YOU ALL FOR LOVING ME AND HELPING ME. I WILL TRY MY BEST TO GROW STRAIGHT AND STRONG IN BODY, MIND AND SPIRIT.

2nd Adult: LET US CLOSE TOGETHER.

Hospitalisation

For all children, being taken into hospital is a lonely and frightening event. When it is their first time away from home it is even more traumatic. But it is a valid Rite of Passage nevertheless, and the effect can be minimised. In some hospitals mothers can stay with the child, but in many cases where the treatment is routine, like an operation for tonsils, adenoids, or appendix, it does mean separation. It is in such moments that the Guardian comes into its own. If a firm contact has been made and the child has been helped and encouraged to build up her Guardian it can become a shield between them and the isolation from home and parents. It is always advisable to reinforce the personality and presence of the protector with a solid image. This might be a homemade felt toy, or perhaps one made in wood, clay, or even a small, silver charm. A picture will do in a small frame hung over the child's bed. A careful child might have a glass or china replica. Dragons, for instance, are obtainable as soft toys, or patterns are sold for making your own.

Breaking the news that time must be spent in the hospital is always tricky, but it can be made easier. Ask if you can take the child in one afternoon to see the ward and meet some of the nurses and children who will be there when they go in. Make sure, however, that the child understands that this time it is just a visit. A sympathetic sister might be asked if their 'lucky emblem' can be kept pinned to the child's pillow, or even allowed with her on the journey to the theatre/tests/x-ray department.

Again the ceremony should be worked the day before, but unlike the first day at school there should be no emphasis on special outings. The tone should be that this is something that lots of people have to do at one time or another and that while it is not very nice, it will be over soon. Of course, if this is not the case then you must prepare the child for a longer stay. A big day-by-day calendar and a thick red pencil to mark off each day will help them to feel that the time is going by more quickly.

The Healing Angel
Parents stand facing each other with the child in between them. One parent performs the opening sequence and the other sends out the Call for the Guardian. Then parents, or parent and friend/grandparent and child sit in a triangle, the two adults behind with the child in front, but close enough to place their hands on her shoulders. Before each one is a lighted candle in a holder. These can be all white, or rose, blue and gold.

Mother: BEHIND ME STANDS GABRIEL, ANGEL OF THE WORD, GIVER OF DREAMS AND ALWAYS THE GUARDIAN OF THE MOTHER AND CHILD. I CALL UPON YOU NOW TO JOIN US HERE AND BRING US PEACE.

Father: BEHIND ME STANDS MICHAEL, WARRIOR ANGEL, PROTECTOR OF THE WEAK. I CALL UPON YOU NOW TO JOIN US HERE AND BRING US COURAGE.

Child: (if old enough, if not then a proxy) BEHIND ME STANDS RAPHAEL THE ANGEL OF Healing, GIVER OF HAPPINESS. I CALL UPON YOU NOW TO JOIN US HERE AND BRING ME HEALING, COURAGE AND PEACE.

Mother: (places hand on child's shoulder) GABRIEL,

ANGEL OF THE MOTHER, PLACE YOUR WINGS ABOUT MY DAUGHTER AND BRING PEACE TO HER HEART. BE WITH HER WHILE SHE IS IN HOSPITAL, GIVE HER DREAMS OF JOY AND HAPPINESS. GIVE HER MEMORIES OF DREAMS SPENT WITH HER AND LET HER MIND BE FILLED WITH CALMNESS DURING THIS TIME OF PASSAGE. LET HER LEARN FROM HER EXPERIENCE AND GROW FROM IT.

Father: (places hand on child's shoulder) MICHAEL, GUARDIAN OF THE GATE OF EDEN, PLACE YOUR WINGS ABOUT MY DAUGHTER AND BRING COURAGE TO HER HEART. HELP HER TO UNDERSTAND THAT THE SEPARATION IS ONLY FOR A LITTLE WHILE AND THAT AFTER SHE WILL BE STRONG AND HEALTHY AGAIN. LET THIS RITE OF PASSAGE BE ONE OF STRENGTH FOR HER. AS SHE EMERGES FROM ITS TEST LET HER BE WISER THAN BEFORE.

Child: RAPHAEL, ANGEL OF HEALING, PLACE YOUR WINGS ABOUT ME AND HELP ME TO BECOME STRONG AND HEALTHY AGAIN. HELP ME TO UNDERSTAND THAT IT WILL ONLY BE FOR A LITTLE WHILE. HELP ME TO BE GRATEFUL FOR THAT WHEN OTHER CHILDREN ARE FAR WORSE THAN MYSELF. HELP ME TO BE STRONG.

Child turns to sit facing her parents and all three candles are placed close together.

Mother: (Child's name), I GIVE YOU MY STRENGTH, AND MY LOVE AS ONCE I GAVE YOU BIRTH.

Father: (Child's name), I GIVE YOU MY STRENGTH AND MY LOVE AS ONCE I GAVE YOU LIFE.

Child: I, (name), GIVE YOU BOTH MY LOVE AND MY PROMISE THAT I WILL BE AS BRAVE AS I CAN, AND THAT I WILL TRY TO LEARN FROM THIS RITE OF PASSAGE.

Silent passive pathworking here with all three looking into the candles' flames. Visualise the three angels standing around the child, their heart centres fully open and rays of green, violet and golden light flowing into the area that needs healing. Build the image of the Guardian standing watch at the edge of the circle, with a small suitcase packed, ready to accompany the child when she leaves for the hospital. Now build images of collecting her from the hospital fully recovered. Spend at least five full minutes on this.

Mother: LET US NOW CLOSE THE CIRCLE AND BLESS THOSE THAT HAVE ANSWERED OUR CALL. I BLESS YOU GABRIEL IN THE NAME OF THAT WHICH CREATED ALL THINGS.

Father: I BLESS YOU MICHAEL IN THE NAME OF THAT WHICH CREATED ALL THINGS.

Child: I BLESS YOU RAPHAEL IN THE NAME OF THE CHILD.

The closing is now performed and the candles are put in a place where they can continue to burn safely for at least another hour. A small picture of an angel drawn and coloured by the child herself can sometimes help to concentrate the mind. Encourage her to continue to build the images of the angels each night before sleeping, speaking to them, asking them for healing and sound sleep. By such methods as this your child will keep her faith in Inner Level beings and the help they can provide, at a time when most other children have already become cynical and closed off from their inner world.

If the child is much too young to join in such a ceremony then the parents and grandparents, friends or even older brothers/sisters, can do it as a healing and protecting ceremony for the child.

The First Time Away From Home and Parents

England has a reputation for using boarding schools even for fairly young children. It was my own greatest fear as a child that I would be sent away to such a school. It is still high on the list of things children fear most. It actually combines two fears in one. The loss of home and all that it means, her own room and bed, toys, books, neighbourhood friends and familiar surroundings. It also means the loss of her parents' company, conversation and the breaking of emotional ties at an age when they are very vulnerable. Homesickness is not something you can 'jolly' a child out of, no matter what the Matron may say!

By no means are all boarding schools Dickensian in outlook, but the effort of looking after so many children in a comparatively narrow age band puts the staff under pressure even in the best of circumstances. There is also the behaviour of children towards each other to consider. While contact with the rough as well as the smooth edges of life is a good thing, some children never get over the shock and revert inwards, sometimes for the rest of their lives. Those who don't, survive by becoming overbearing, a condition which often hides a lot of pain. A few make it through without too much trouble.

The first time away may be at Summer Camp, or holidaying with friends who live at the other end of the country or even overseas. It may be a school skiing holiday or a tutorial cruise to the isles of Greece. The first time away from home is truly a Rite of Passage. Even quite young children are appalled at the thought of dressing and undressing in front of others, and communal showers can be a nightmare. Also, by this time, the child may be feeling sensitive about having a Guardian, but reluctant to give it up completely. This is the time to reveal that a simple picture, or even a felt cut-out, can embody the protector as easily as the toy image. The child may even have acquired the skill to use a projected image and outgrown the need for the friend and protector of her early childhood. If so then this is the time for her to learn how to summon a *Companion of Light*. The ritual has been written for the child to work without help, although if need be a parent can help out.

What is a Companion of Light? It is similar in kind to the invisible companions children often acquire by themselves when very young. It may be chosen from one of the Angelic Choirs. If so I would favour one of the Cherubim, the angels of Yesod. They are called 'The Strong Ones', a fitting title for a Companion. Or try one of the Ashim, the angels of Malkuth. If this is not suitable then use a thoughtform ensouled by an angelic. This combines the best of both 'worlds', say a young Faun, or a Centaur, a fairy creature, or simply just another child looking some three or four years older than the child herself to give the necessary feeling of comfort and protection.

Once the form has been chosen the child must become thoroughly familiar with it. If she has the skill, get her to draw it; if not, then look through books for something similar and photocopy it, paste the picture inside a notebook, diary, or put it into a picture wallet. Sit with her daily, close your eyes and build the image together until it becomes 'real'. The giving of a name is important. The image must become as real to the parent(s) as it is to the child. They must acknowledge its presence and believe in its creation as a companion and protector for their daughter. This building may take as long as a month or more, but when the Companion's name becomes as familiar in conversation as that of the family pet it is time to use the ritual.

You will need a mirror, four white candles that have been previously prepared with anointing oil, the picture of the Companion, and a small bell (the kind they put on cats collars), some oil of Rosemary and an oil burner.

Calling the Companion
Place the candles at the four quarters on the floor with a cushion in front of each one. Light the burner and put on a few drops of Rosemary oil. Light the candles, with a whispered blessing of the angel of each quarter (if using an angelic companion). Raphael for the East, Michael for the South, Gabriel for the West and Uriel or Sandalphon for the North. As much of all this as possible should be done by the child herself. If using a thoughtform, invoke the Elemental Kings as well as the Angelics: Paralda for the East, Djinn for the South, Nixsa for the West and Ghob for the North. I have *not* advised the use of an elemental to animate the thoughtform as they can be unpredictable and, because of their nature, they cannot tell right from wrong until they have been trained themselves. Not until the child is old enough to make a reliable judgement herself can they be used.

Next comes the Opening and the Call to the Guardian who has a right to be there to be blessed and 'retired'. Now the ceremony begins.

Child: THE TIME HAS COME TO RELEASE YOU (Guardian's name) FROM YOUR ROLE AS GUARDIAN. NOW YOU ARE FREE TO REST AND THEN TO TAKE UP

THE TASK OF GUARDING ANOTHER YOUNG CHILD. (at this point the Guardian may be passed ceremoniously to a younger sibling) WE BLESS YOU TO THE FULL AMOUNT YOU ARE ABLE TO RECEIVE IN THE NAME OF THAT WHICH CREATED US ALL. YOU ARE WELCOME IN THIS FAMILY AS AN HONOURED FRIEND ON THE INNER LEVELS.

All: WE NOW COME TOGETHER TO BUILD THE ASTRAL FORM OF THE COMPANION OF LIGHT.

Now follows a spoken visualisation along the lines of the following:

Child: MY NEW COMPANION IS A FAUN. HE/SHE IS ABOUT TWO OR THREE YEARS OLDER THAN MYSELF, AND ABOUT FOUR INCHES TALLER.

Adult: THE FAUN HAS A GOLDEN-BROWN SKIN, AND THE GOAT LEGS ARE COVERED WITH FINE SILKY LIGHT BROWN HAIR WHICH IS KEPT VERY CLEAN AND WELL-BRUSHED. THE HOOVES ARE POLISHED AND NEATLY CLIPPED.

Child: THE EARS ARE POINTED AND HAVE SMALL TUFTS OF HAIR ON THE POINT ITSELF. THE EYES ARE HAZEL WITH FLECKS OF GREEN AND SLANT A LITTLE. HIS/HER VOICE IS LIGHT AND MUSICAL AND HE/SHE HAS A NICE LAUGH, WARM AND VERY FRIENDLY.

Adult: THE FAUN HAS CERTAIN MAGICAL POWERS, ENOUGH TO PROTECT MY CHILD FROM THOSE DANGERS THAT EVERY CHILD FACES. BUT WHERE ORDINARY EVERYDAY EXPERIENCES MEANT TO TEACH AND INFORM ARE CONCERNED, THE FAUN WILL STAND BY AND ONLY ACT IF THINGS GO WRONG. IF NEEDS BE, THE FAUN IS GRANTED POWER TO CALL FOR GREATER FORCE THAN ITSELF TO PROTECT AND COMFORT.

Child: THE FAUN'S NAME IS .... AND HE/SHE COMES TO BE MY COMPANION UNTIL SUCH TIME AS I MUST TAKE RESPONSIBILITY FOR MYSELF IN ALL THINGS. HE/SHE BRINGS A SMALL SUITCASE IN WHICH CAN BE FOUND THE FOLLOWING ITEMS. A THICK SWEATER FOR THE COLD WEATHER, A BATH TOWEL, A WASHBAG WITH SOAP, TOOTHBRUSH AND TOOTHPASTE. A COMB AND A BRUSH AND ANOTHER HARDER BRUSH FOR

CLEANING HOOVES. A TIN OF POLISH AND A POLISHING CLOTH ALSO FOR THE HOOVES. A FOLDING UMBRELLA, A PICTURE OF GREAT PAN, AND A SET OF PIPES. I CALL YOU .... BY YOUR NAME. I WELCOME YOU AS MY COMPANION OF LIGHT. (stands in East, picks up the Mirror and looks into it)

MY NAME IS .... AND I INVOKE THE POWER OF THE EAST, THE POWER OF LIGHT AND OF ILLUMINATION TO FILL MY COMPANION THAT IT MAY BETTER SUSTAIN ME. I CALL UPON RAPHAEL AND PARALDA TO MAKE THIS SO. (visualises Companion behind her being touched and filled with golden Light. Child moves to Southern candle, looks into Mirror)

MY NAME IS .... AND I INVOKE THE POWER OF THE SOUTH, THE POWER OF PROTECTION AND LOYALTY TO FILL MY COMPANION THAT IT MAY BETTER SHIELD ME FROM HARM. I CALL UPON MICHAEL AND DJINN TO MAKE THIS SO. (visualises Companion as before, moves to Western candle and looks into mirror)

MY NAME IS .... AND I INVOKE THE POWER OF THE WEST, THE POWER OF KNOWLEDGE AND INTUITION TO FILL MY COMPANION THAT IT MAY BETTER INFORM AND ADVISE ME. I CALL UPON GABRIEL AND NIXSA TO MAKE THIS SO. (visualises the Companion as before, then moves to Northern candle and looks into mirror)

MY NAME IS .... AND I INVOKE THE POWER OF THE NORTH, THE POWER OF COMFORT AND ENDURANCE TO FILL MY COMPANION THAT IT MAY BETTER COMFORT AND SOOTHE ME. I CALL UPON URIEL AND GHOB TO MAKE THIS SO. (returns to East)

AS I HAVE SAID, SO IT WILL BE.

Adult: (takes picture of Companion, wets the back of it with spittle) WITH MY OWN SUBSTANCE I BEGIN THE EMPOWERMENT OF THE COMPANION AND ADD MY POWER AS THE MOTHER/FATHER TO THAT OF THE ANGELIC AND ELEMENTAL POWERS. (takes picture to each quarter and lets a small drop of candle wax fall on the back of the picture)

IT IS DONE. LET US CLOSE.

Allow a few days for the Companion to fully assimilate the

power. From then the child should make a point of acknowledging it by name or in conversation each day at least once and preferably three times: on waking, at noon, and before sleeping. Like the Guardian, the Companion may be blessed and released when the child no longer has need of it.

Death

Death is something we cannot avoid and it is a mistake to try and protect children from its existence. I have already said, children understand far more than we think, and Death touches us on many levels: that of a parent, a grandparent, a friend and, of course, ourselves. Often, the first time a child comes into contact with this natural event is when a pet dies. Sometimes they are born into a family where there is already a pet, or a pet is acquired when they begin to grow. As the pet gets visibly older it can be explained to the child that the cat or dog can no longer play or roughhouse or walk as far as before. Like Grandad, it is no longer young and full of energy, it must rest and sleep more often and needs to be quiet.

Tell the child frankly that the life expectancy of animals is shorter than ours, but that because they experience life in a different way they get as much out of the shorter span as we do from living longer. This should be said right from the moment you think about obtaining a pet animal. Prepare them for the loss ahead of time: '. . . our old friend is getting close to the time when he will have to leave us and return to the Group Soul of the Great Dog/Cat, etc. Tell her about Group Souls being the repository of all the souls of that species, unless an animal has been so loved, so much a part of the family that it has become partly individualised. In this case it will go back to the Group Soul for a while to pass on its experience of life, and then after resting may return either in another body, or to wait until it is time to greet us when we die.

I realise that those of an orthodox belief may feel unable to speak in this way, but children form great attachments to animals and should be allowed the comforting thought of their continuation after death. The sudden disappearance of a pet with no explanation is cruel and unnecessary. If the animal has to be put down even a fairly young child can understand that it is hurting too much to get better and sending it back to the Great Cat or the Great Dog is better than keeping it in pain. Many vets now offer cremation for pets, so the ashes can be scattered over a favourite spot. There are also a few pet cemeteries where the old companion can be laid to rest, but usually it is the garden or a quiet spot on a favourite walk. The child will usually wish to participate and should be allowed to do so. It is also important that they be allowed to mourn their friend.

Losing a friend, especially one of their own age, can be especially traumatic for a child. It rocks the foundation of their own life expectancy, it is so close to home. It is a sad fact of life that some children do die young, sometimes in ways and in circumstances that can cause deep shock to their peers. Traffic accidents, air disasters, the onset of incurable diseases, murders and incidents where an adult goes berserk with a shotgun are, unfortunately, part of life in the twentieth century. Living through the Battle of Britain as I did, one learned to cope by withdrawing, by not making friendships too deep or too meaningful. It did not lessen the hurt and the fear, but it enabled one to go on living. Grief counselling is now an accepted and vital part of such events. Never think that because they are young, 'they will forget and get over it'. Encourage them to talk, do not shut the incident away. This allows them to keep the image and the memory alive and to let time gently disintegrate it when they are ready to let go.

The death of a grandparent is often felt deeply, there is a bond between grandchild and grandparent that is unique. If it is possible, let the child visit often as their life draws to a close, remind them that at anytime this person that they love will close their eyes and go away. They will not be able to follow yet. By allowing them to be a part of the moment you also show them that death can be a gentle release from pain and weariness.

The death of a parent leaves an enormous gap in the life of a young child, and even into the teen years. It requires a lot of sensitivity from those around to ease this terrible Rite of Passage. Do not shut the dead away, talk about them, recall past moments, times you shared, let the child know you remember them. Above all, allow them to mourn. Yes, we believe that they have gone ahead to a place of beauty and peace, but there is no doubt that we would rather have them here, with us. The following rituals allow for both these feelings to surface. With regard to the needs of older children and adults, allow me to direct you to my book *The New Book of the Dead* (Aquarian 1992), for further rituals dealing with death.

The Death of a Pet

If the animal is to be buried in the garden or some selected spot, allow the child to see the animal's body *if she so wishes*. Do not force this upon her however. A body bag can be obtained from the vet, or two black polythene bags one inside the other will be needed. Arrange the animal's limbs before they stiffen. The child can say goodbye to her friend and sprinkle flowers and herbs (Rosemary, Thyme, Bay and Lavender are the best to use) over the body before the bag is sealed. A favourite toy, ball, or plaything may also be placed with the animal at this time. It used to be that in past centuries, a dog was buried at his master's feet to accompany him into the beyond, so that he would not go alone and friendless. A small photograph of the child and pet together is one way of following this ancient tradition.

Place the body somewhere away from the house, but where the child can simply go and sit if she wishes. The evening before or just prior to the animal's burial a remembrance ceremony can be held. The same opening can be used and the Guardian can be summoned to act as a guide over the Bridge between Life and Death.

Adult: WE HAVE COME TO SAY GOODBYE TO A DEAR FRIEND AND COMPANION, ONE WHO GAVE US LOVE, AFFECTION AND LOYALTY FOR MANY YEARS. THE PASSING OF (pet's name) WILL LEAVE A BIG GAP IN OUR LIVES, ONE THAT CAN NEVER BE REALLY FILLED. WE HAVE MANY MEMORIES OF (pet's name)'S YOUNG DAYS, OF TIMES WHEN WE WERE PERHAPS LESS THAN LOVING, OF TIMES WHEN WE HAD FUN TOGETHER. WE LEARNED A LOT FROM BEING WITH YOU. WE HOPE

THAT YOU LEARNED FROM BEING WITH US. WHEN YOU
RETURN TO YOUR GROUP SOUL WE HOPE THAT IT WILL
LEARN FROM YOU THAT NOT ALL HUMANS ARE CRUEL
AND THOUGHTLESS, THAT SOME ARE LOVING AND
KIND AND GRATEFUL FOR THE UNDEMANDING LOVE
AND COMPANIONSHIP THAT OUR YOUNGER
BRETHREN OFFER TO US. WE ALSO HOPE THAT ONE
DAY, WHEN IT IS OUR TIME TO PASS OVER THE BRIDGE,
WE WILL SEE A FAMILIAR SHAPE WAITING FOR US ON
THE OTHER SIDE.

THANK YOU (pet's name). BLESS YOU IN EVERY WAY.
MAY THE GUARDIAN TAKE YOU SAFELY ACROSS THE
BRIDGE.

Child: I WANT TO THANK YOU (pet's name) FOR
GROWING UP WITH ME, FOR PLAYING WITH ME AND
TEACHING ME MANY THINGS. HOW TO CARE FOR YOU,
HOW TO KEEP YOU WELL AND HEALTHY AND HAPPY.
I AM SORRY IF I EVER HURT YOU OR GAVE YOU CAUSE
TO BE UNHAPPY. I WILL REMEMBER YOU WITH LOVE
AND IF ANOTHER ANIMAL COMES INTO MY LIFE, IT
WILL NOT TAKE YOUR PLACE, BUT WILL MAKE ITS OWN
PLACE IN MY HEART. BECAUSE OF YOU I WILL KNOW
BETTER HOW TO CARE FOR IT AND ONE DAY I WILL
TEACH MY OWN CHILDREN WHAT YOU TAUGHT ME. I
KNOW THAT YOU ARE NOW BEGINNING A JOURNEY
YOU MUST TRAVEL ALONE, BUT THE GUARDIAN WILL
SEE YOU SAFELY ACROSS AND TO YOUR GROUP SOUL.
IF IT IS ALLOWED, AND IF YOU WISH TO DO SO, PLEASE
RETURN TO US IN A NEW BODY. IF THIS CANNOT
HAPPEN, THEN I WILL LOOK FOR YOU WHEN I CROSS
THE BRIDGE ONE DAY IN THE FUTURE. GUARDIAN,
ATTEND. TAKE THE SPIRIT OF (pet's name) AND GO WITH
HER/HIM ACROSS THE BRIDGE OF LIFE AND DEATH.
TAKE HIM/HER ALL THE WAY TO THE GROUP SOUL,
AND DON'T FORGET THE TOYS AND THE PHOTOGRAPH
SO (pet's name) WILL REMEMBER ME. GOODBYE (pet's
name). BLESS YOU AND THANK YOU.

After this the burial may take place and a small bush or
sapling planted as a memorial of your companion. The
essence of the animal may return or be felt around for a few

days, or even longer if the tie has been strong. But it will gradually fade. The finest compliment one can pay to such a friend is to offer a loving home to another of its species when the time feels right. Do not do this too soon or the child may feel some antagonism towards the newcomer and the animal will suffer rejection. Allow time to close the gap.

Death of a Friend/Relative/Parent

This is more complex and will depend on how the death occurred. There will of course be a formal funeral which the child may attend if not too young or too easily upset. My personal belief is that the private farewell is best done in the form of a Pathworking or Guided Meditation rather than as a ritual. This allows the projected image to interact with the child and also has the effect of helping to release any emotional feelings that have been dammed up as a result of grief or shock.

It is also a way in which, if circumstances have been such that the child has not been able to say 'goodbye', she can take her leave of a loved one and be allowed that time together. There is also the very real possibility that the spirit of the relative, especially if the tie has been a close one, will for a few moments ensoul the image and this will allow them both to release their grief and say au revoir.

This pathworking *must* be done with an adult taking an active part in the procedure. Over the age of about twelve I would say a lot depends upon the type of child, but I personally would prefer that a close and well-liked relative was near to hand.

Make sure the room is quiet and safe from intrusion, with tissues to hand, and a thermos of hot tea with plenty of sugar, and some plain biscuits to help the closing of the psychic centres afterwards. This is important. It is also important that the pathworking is not prepared for, the child should not be told that it *will* take place at a certain time. Ask, as if on the spur of the moment, if the child would like to say goodbye by means of a pathworking, that it is something you would like to do and you thought she might like to 'go' with you. If as yet she has no idea what a pathworking is, explain. If she is used to them she will understand right away. (Incidentally, this method of dealing with grief can be used by anyone at any age.)

Goodbye is Not Forever

Sit side by side and, if it is comfortable to do so, hold hands. In your other hand hold a photograph of the deceased; preferably a photo showing you both together. Breathe deeply and easily, close your eyes and begin to build up the image of the person as you remember him/her best. Take your time and build it in detail. If you like you may build the image as it appears in the photo. When the image is as clear and detailed as you can possibly get it signal to the person with you by squeezing their hand. Wait until they signal their own readiness by returning the pressure.

Greet the image as you would if they were really with you, image yourself going forward and holding them, kissing them. Then watch the other person join you. Beyond you is a soft white mist and the three of you, holding hands, walk forward into it and through it. As you do so it melts away and you find yourselves in a country lane with the person you love and thought you would never see again. They are well and strong and happy, smiling at you and looking as you remember them. You all begin to walk down the lane.

At first just walk, look around you and take note of your surroundings. You might find them familiar, it may be a place you often visited, or somewhere that holds a special meaning for you. Your subconscious mind may have found it in your memories. The lane twists and turns, and across the hedges on either side you can get glimpses of woods on one side and cliffs with a footpath on the other. A little further along you come to a gate leading into a field of ripening corn. It is almost waist high and along the edge runs a narrow path. It leads across the field and over a stile into another lane, but this is a private lane and takes you to a white gate opening onto a thatched cottage, with an old-fashioned garden full of flowers. Just stand for a moment and smell the air, try to tell which flowers are there by their scent. Roses certainly, and Pinks, Sweet Williams and Snapdragons. Hollyhocks stand at the very back with Golden Rod and Lupins in front.

The door stands open and at the side of the cottage is a wooden trestle table with a wooden bench alongside. The person you have come to see asks you to sit down and goes inside to bring out a tray of sandwiches, homemade scones with strawberry jam and cream. There is tea in the pot and chinaware of a deep pansy blue, edged with a band of gold. Now you can begin to eat and drink and share this time with the person you love and thought you had lost. They reassure you that they are just as alive now as they ever were, but in a different kind of way. They feel real to you – put out your hand and touch them. Talk to them using your real voice if you like, they will answer you. Don't distress them by telling them you want them to come back, they cannot do that and you must accept it for a fact. What you can do is to understand that, for a while you can meet them in this way, talk to them, share your grief and talk about your dreams and hopes with them. You will not want to believe it now, but in time you will need to use this way of meeting less and less, then there will be a time when you can say 'goodbye' and let them go.

But for now, finish your tea and then get up, kiss them and tell them you will see them soon. You all walk down to the gate and two of you only step beyond it and walk down the lane, turn and wave, and when you turn again you walk into the mist and come back into your own present time.

Allow a few minutes to collect your thoughts and feelings, then have something to eat and drink and close down. Write down if you wish what you have experienced and keep a diary until the day when you will meet in the lane for the last time.

The first few times you will come back crying. This is natural, so don't try to hold it back. Tears are healing in such circumstances. You can vary the location if you like and meet them elsewhere, but keep the cottage at the back of your mind as a peaceful retreat from loneliness and sorrow.

This working will act just as well for young wives and husbands who have lost partners, parents who have lost children. It is gentle, not stressful at all, and can ease much of your burden.

PART 2
SPRING
The Maiden Years

4

THE FIRST FLOWING

Somewhere between the ages of about twelve and thirteen the most important Rite of Passage in a girl's life will occur: the first Menstruation. It is seldom an unexpected thing nowadays, very few young girls are left totally unaware of what to expect. Spare a thought for the old days when girls would suddenly find themselves covered in blood, ashamed and embarrassed, convinced they were dying of some dreadful disease or, in some ways even worse, had committed some dire sin and were being punished.

At least today it is not a topic that is taboo between mother and daughter. Yet, there are *still* taboos going on in the home, even now. I have been told of families where the father will not eat at the same table when mother or daughters are '. . . in that dirty condition' and homes where the daughters are warned to hide any soiled underwear immediately so their father and brother will not be offended. There are still religions that teach a woman that she is *unclean and polluted* during this special time. Most of them are religions that still practise female circumcision.

Daughters of Eve, this book is being written for you, listen to me well, there is nothing unclean or wrong or dirty about you during your period. It is a sign that your body is doing its job and doing it well. Yes, it may for some of you be a painful time, in which case seek help from your doctor or go to a clinic or an alternative practitioner and ask for advice and help. You do not have to suffer in this way. *But you are not unclean.* What is happening? Quite simple.

Your body has become mature enough (by biological standards) to conceive and carry to term, a child. You will certainly not be ready emotionally or psychologically, but your body and your mind will differ on that point for a while yet. Each month an egg, or ovum, will begin to travel from one of your ovaries down through the Fallopian tube to the uterus. There it will wait patiently to be fertilised by a passing male sperm or, in point of fact, it will wait to be hassled by several millions of the little tikes. Like a good Girl Guide it will prepare for its hypothetical guest by laying down a coating in the womb that will, if the ova is fertilised, become the placenta. When nothing happens it will no doubt shrug its shoulders and murmur 'c'est la vie', and prepare to vacate the premises. While it is doing this it also very tidily clears away the prepared coating, and you have a period which clears and cleans the womb and makes it ready for the next time. That, basically, is all that a period is about.

The female womb is eternally hopeful and very house-proud, it will go on, barring accidents, pregnancies and disease, continuing to prepare the 'guest room' every month from now until you reach your menopause, which varies in onset from between the mid forties to the late fifties. I was 58 when mine decided to shut up shop. Even my doctor was beginning to wonder when it would stop.

If you think of it in these terms you will realise that the analogy of the houseproud lady preparing to welcome a special guest, or maybe an unexpected guest, is very apt. Most women with a spare room will keep it clean and bright, with a set of fresh, pretty sheets and soft plumped-up pillows always ready in case someone comes to stay. In the case of a pregnancy, if they do, the room becomes occupied for a while, nine months in fact, then the guest leaves and the room is empty. It needs to be cleaned and all traces of its occupant taken away, then made ready in case another one comes along. (See chapter 7 for a ritual concerning this cleansing.)

Sometimes the guest room is never occupied because of circumstances that are still beyond medical control. This can cause great sorrow to some women, while others have little or no maternal instinct. They are no less feminine for this. It is a fallacy that every single woman wants to be a mother. Some do and are, some wish and can't, some won't and don't.

This time in your life also coincides with adolescence, a time when you are liable to be a trial to your parents, siblings, yourself and everyone around you. To be fair, it's not your fault. Your hormones are racing around your system like a Ferrari at Brands Hatch. This is a time of deep despairing days alternated with wildly joyful moments, mixed with moods darker than a coal mine at midnight. Combine this with a tendency to spots, weight fluctuation, school exams, and crushes on various pop stars and you can see that the Maiden Years are not exactly the high spot of your life. However, once in a while some lucky young woman sails through this emotional slalom course with an unblemished complexion, a model figure, a sweet smile and a happy nature. She does have one problem though – all the other girls hate her guts!

Even during your darkest times, usually when your father has prised the phone out of your hand for the tenth time and threatened to have it cut off (the phone not the hand), there is hope. You DO grow out of it, there IS an end to adolescence. One morning the household wakes up to find a sweet-natured, gentle-voiced young woman amongst them and the worst is over. Before this happens, though, you will run the gamut of emotions on most days, bring your parents to the edge of divorce, and may even cause the dog to leave home.

Among other things you will feel deserted and misunderstood, spend miserable nights crying into your pillow and, if you are normal, may indulge in weepy fantasies that revolve around you lying on your death bed (well, almost – you'll always make a miraculous recovery) with your mother begging you to try to *live*, so you *can* wear the slinky black number she bought in Harrods sale and says is too old for you. Your father will promise on his knees that you can have your *very own phone*, if only you will get well again. The teenager has not yet been born who has not indulged in some kind of daydream at some time or other. Enjoy them, they are good for your sore self image and they are one way of calming down.

You are emotionally very vulnerable at this time and can easily fall prey to the male of species who is going through his own adolescent purgatory. Because he is behind you mentally by at least three years he has even less control over his hormones than you have. Both sexes cling together in groups for mutual self esteem, both can erupt into violence if self discipline has not been part of your upbringing. This

is the time to learn and understand that the male ego is a
fragile blossom and never more so than in the very young and
the newly middle aged. Taunts and barbs can drive them past
endurance and you can be badly hurt, physically, emotionally
and mentally if you drive them too far.

This is often the time when you feel you are old enough to
experiment with sex. Maybe you are, but . . . stop and think
about it. Psychically speaking, sexual intercourse forms what
is called an Arc Thread between two people. This is the term
used to describe that subtle astral link that is formed by and
through the sexual act. Left alone, they will eventually
dissolve and fall away unless renewed by further contact.
Then they get stronger. It can act as a cord binding together
people who have outgrown each other and want to part, but
find they cannot do it as easily as they thought.

Sex is not an amusement, it is not something to indulge in
because there is nothing on at the cinema. It is, Daughter of
Eve, one of the great Sacraments.

It is a Ritual of great power in and of itself when used in
the right way. As a woman, even though as yet a young and
untried woman, you must learn to think of yourself as a
Chalice, a Grail, that will contain, for the right man, the
essence that will make of him a complete Man. Without you,
he cannot achieve that. Together you are the Cup and the
Athame, the Sword and the Scabbard, the Lock and the Key.

There is an occult tradition held for thousands of years, that
to be the first to taste the wine of a Virgin Chalice, more
specifically a trained Chalice, endows that man/priest with
great power. It was this power that enroyalled the Pharoah
when he married a princess of the Blood Royal. It was for this
reason that Henry Tudor had to marry the young Elizabeth
of York. Without her position as the holder of the Power of the
Land he could not, in the eyes of his people, become Henry
VII of England. Every untouched woman holds that same
power. A young woman entering a convent with a true
vocation, brings her virgin power to the altar and enriches the
whole church. That is what sets her apart. We may look on
it today as an anachronism, but the church knows the power
of such a sacrifice.

Virginity is little valued in this world today, yet it still holds
an ancient power. *Do not throw it away.* It is a gift that can be

given only once and never again. Given to the right person, at the right moment and for the right reasons, it becomes the Crown of the Inner Kingdom for both of you. It is the moment when the Empress makes the Fool into the Emperor and places the sceptre of sovereignty in his hand.

These strange, fiery, emotional years are full of pain and wonder, yet they are preparing you for the rest of your life. Childhood is now, for this incarnation at least, behind you. Before you is an unknown land called maturity. Don't hurry through these years, try to learn from the lessons they impose on you. If you are planning a university education, enjoy it. It is a unique time and one which will give you many memories to store for your older years. You may wish to start work. If so, no matter what it is, give your best to it – the rewards may surprise you. Whatever you decide to do with your life, remember this is a time of change. The ambition of your life may change overnight into something totally its opposite. Flow with it, like your First Flowing. Remember the guest room prepared each month – well, life can be like that. If you prepare yourself to receive whatever chances may come your way at a moment's notice, it may well flower into something that will fill your life.

If nothing comes, then sweep away old ideas and look for new ones. Every now and then take stock of your life and see what can be thrown away and what can be turned around, and what is available that is new and exciting.

Make the start of each month a time for a new idea. Make each year a time for trying out a new way or a new pattern to your life. Even when something comes along that satisfies you enough to stay with it, remember that it can always be looked at with new eyes after a time. Nothing is so good that it cannot be improved. Nothing is so bad that you cannot use some part of it.

Learn to use talismanic magic. Menstrual blood is not unclean, it is a totally pure substance, in fact it is pre-placental material which in the natural course of pregnancy would be the prime source of food for a baby. All the nutrients the child needs come from the mother's bloodstream through the placenta and on to the child via the umbilical cord. Menstrual blood is a very primal and powerful part of your body, and it holds creative and magical power of a high order.

Used to seal a sigil or Talisman, to anoint an amulet or candle for magical purposes, or to link you magically with a sacred site or location, it can increase your female power of connection a hundredfold. The ancients knew this and it is one of many reasons why men who, untrained or bound by social conventions, are afraid of it, and of any woman in her moon phase. Those men who know and understand and who can see and honour the power in a woman at these times can truly be called Moon Priests.

If the blood is used it should be used fresh as its power soon wanes like the Moon herself. At this time any woman is at the very peak of her power and also at her most feminine. It is a time when many women are banned from entering Holy Places in other Traditions. The old cliché that your body is a Temple is quite true – it is, but that saying has been used so often and so badly that it has become overlooked and underestimated.

Your body is, in truth, a Temple, a Church, a Cathedral, a Holy Place. It should be kept clean and fragrant and nowhere more than the Sacred Way that lies, guarded, behind the feminine triangle. The way lies between the Two Pillars of your thighs and hidden by the sacred bush. The Outer and the Inner Veils of the labia, when drawn apart, reveal the entrance to the Cave of the Hidden Goddess. It is also called the Cave of Stars, and it has a Guardian, the female clitoris to whom homage must be paid before proceeding along the sacred way. Your womb is that part of the Temple that is withdrawn, the Holy of Holies, the Adytum, the Sanctuary where the Grail is kept. Only you have the right to grant entry, and then only for a time. Even a child is granted sanctuary for just nine months, then it must leave. This place is where YOUR WOMAN'S SACRED POWER HAS ITS SOURCE. Never forget that, Daughter of Eve. Millions of women have died in the flames, of persecution to protect the knowledge that you may now learn freely. Bless their name in every prayer you utter. They deserve your respect.

5

FIRST LOVE,
LOOSING THE KESTOS

In Shakespeare's *Romeo and Juliet*, when her parents are discussing the possibility of their daughter's betrothal, Juliet's mother remarks that '. . . she hath but fourteen summers'. To which her father answers, somewhat testily, '. . . younger than she are happy mothers made . . .'. In the fourteenth century, a lonely and probably frightened little French princess of eleven, married to a Prince of Spain, received a letter from her mother exhorting her to grow quickly into a woman and get herself with child as speedily as possible. No loving inquiries as to whether or not she was homesick, was she eating well and getting enough exercise . . . just a curt note telling her to grow up, now!

You might think you live in a more enlightened age, Daughter of Eve. You are not expected to marry for expediency or to bear children at an age when you should be enjoying your own childhood. But, the world being what it is, there are still child marriages in India and Africa and many other places. In Britain and in America there are still thirteen and fourteen year olds getting pregnant and bearing children and, unless they are very lucky in their parents, having to give them away for adoption. This can lead to a life of bitterness and regret.

Love is a fragile thing. It needs constant attention if it is to last into the Golden Years, and constant attention is sometimes hard to give. There will be times, many times, when your hormones will let rip and yell, 'okay . . . now hear this . . . he is the one and only'. There is only one snag with hormones – they are great liars and they tend to cry wolf a lot. Then one day when they yell you take no notice and miss the chance of a lifetime. Love is a tough thing to handle. But you owe it to yourself to be choosy. Did you realise that you are unique, that there will never, ever, be someone just like you? That being the case you deserve the best, so go looking. But take it slow.

'Love don't come easy', says the song, and you'd better believe it. Real life is not a Mills and Boon paperback, it is far more complex than that, but the one point of reference you can rely upon is that men, all men, mature more slowly than women mentally and emotionally. Physically they reach their sexual peak between eighteen and twenty-four. After that they tire easily!

By contrast, YOU, Daughter of Eve, will reach your sexual maturity around forty and be rarin' to go for the next twenty years. Even after that, the fires don't die down – not every seventy year old is as quiet as she looks. You have all the time in the world to look, touch, taste and try out. You do not have to get it all in one fell swoop.

First Love

Nothing is quite so wonderful or so painful as your first love. You will never forget him, he will always have a place in your heart. He may have been eight years old with dental braces, or sixteen, skinny and dedicated to the God of Acne, but he was the first one that made your heart beat faster and caused sleepless nights and tear-dampened pillows. Your first kiss may have been a sloppy, misdirected nose-squashing failure, but it *was* your first. Your first real date, with a new dress, new hairdo and a borrowed padded bra is a memory you will treasure all your days. They are sweet and slightly bitter, these memories, because they come only once. The second love, the second kiss, the dates that come after; all these will fade in time, but the first will keep shining in your mind like a beacon. And they *are* beacons, lights that lit the way into your maiden years with so many new things to discover and to experience. It was and is a whole new world.

Does love come more than once? Yes, it does, and some say it is best the second time around. In the early years of this fast-fading century there was a musical comedy called *The Maid of the Mountains*. It contained a song that achieved great popularity at the time, and the lyrics fit this part of the book perfectly.

> When he fancies he is past love,
> it is then he meets his last love,
> and he loves her as he's never loved before.
> (The Maid of the Mountains. Music by James Tate Libretto: Harris and Valentine. Copyright EMI)

At the time of our first love we think that there will never be another one. On very rare occasions that may be true, but for the most part we will love many times during our lives. Those loves will be different – more, or sometimes less, intense. For some passion will run high and fast, for others there will come the deep, quiet love that outlasts life itself. It is quite possible to love two or even three men at the same time for very different aspects of their personalities. It makes one wonder sometimes why polyandry never really caught on, when polygamy did and is still allowed in many areas of the world.

If and when your first wild, sweet love finally fades, don't let yourself fall into the slough of despondence and tell yourself that you will never love again. You will, again and again and again. It is normal and right that you should. ninety-nine point nine per cent of people do. Occasionally there are couples for whom the first is the only one, but they are rare. Cry your fill if you must, but hold in the back of your mind that there will be another love for you when the time is right.

What makes people fall in love with one person and not with another who may be more suitable mentally, emotionally, socially and even financially? Well, we really do not know the full answer to this. What we do know is that everyone has their own body perfume. We also know it is a scent that is theirs alone and that it can interact with that of other people in a way that attracts them to each other. These pheromones or particles of odour are extremely powerful and although, as animals, we have lost most of our ability to trace by scent, we still retain enough for the sense of smell to be one of the most powerful influences in our lives. The male moth will fly many miles in one night to answer the scented call of a female. This is not so very different from the human male who will drive, also for miles, to keep a date with his girl friend. If he doesn't give her scented flowers, he may well tell her that her perfume drives him crazy, which of course it is designed to do. Be careful in your choice, though, as what turns one man on may well turn another right off.

This chemical reaction to members of the opposite sex makes us even more aware, if we had forgotten it, that we must also be classed as 'animals'. However, unlike animals, a human female has a monthly fertile cycle instead of a sexual season just once a year. Also, her sexual response is not limited to that special season, but only by her own decision, feelings, and needs.

Loosing the Kestos

Falling in love does not always mean falling into sex as well. Often first love is the purest you will ever know, something that grows out of looks, touches, sighs, a few words and fewer experiences. It can be a shy love that may never progress beyond dreams, or it can lead on to something that will change you forever, something that will colour your idea of love and sex, for good or bad, for the rest of your life. Therefore it is not something to do without thought, or simply because 'it's a bore to be a virgin, and all the other girls have done it . . .', etc, etc.

The loosing of the Kestos is a sacred act, whether or not you choose to see it as such. The Kestos was the sacred girdle or belt that was bound about the waist and hips of the sacred virgins of the temple – those whose purity of blood, combined with their trained skills as pythonesses or seers, made them highly-valued members of the Mysteries. Their destiny was that of the heirosgamos or sacred marriage with the high priests, or with someone whose psychic talents matched their own. It was in this way that the arcane abilities were handed on to the next generation, in rather the same way that there are arranged marriages in parts of the world today.

At the onset of menstruation a decorative belt was placed

about the waist and from then on no man might touch them unless by permission. The only man who might 'loosen the Kestos' was the one destined to be empowered by their once in a lifetime gift. The power flow was not one way either: in the giving the little priestess also received and passed through the next Gate of Womanhood. Often she went on to become the High Priestess herself. Such women were honoured and held in sacred awe throughout the Mediterranean and middle-Eastern cultures of the past.

When the time comes for you to confer your 'gift' on the man of your choice, let it be because there is something in your relationship that will make it unique. If you have kept your 'gift' until marriage you will be in the very special position of giving your husband something that is a once-in-a-lifetime moment of empowerment. If you are marrying someone who is aware of the magical side of things, then together you can make it far more than a mere sexual uniting, it can become a true Sacrament, a sacred marriage similar to the ancient heirosgamos. If he is unaware of the situation then you can tune into the spiritual nature of the mating without him knowing, but he will still be gifted by its power, providing you wish this to be so. If not, then there is a way of keeping the power for yourself, as you will see later in this chapter.

Once the hymen is broken nothing can physically bring it back, the power of it has gone. So what if the unthinkable happens and your virginity is lost through a sexual assault, a rape?

Listen and listen well, Daughter of Eve. Valuable and potent though it is, your life is worth more than your purity. If you have even the slightest notion that your life is in danger, give in, allow it to happen. DO NOT FIGHT in such a situation. You could get badly injured or lose your life. If you simply allow it to happen you will avoid the kind of internal injuries that might be incurred by resisting the forcing of the penis into your unready and untried body.

If a woman is prepared by a man for her first mating, with loving hands and gentle words, the moment when the hymen is broken is no more than a moment's discomfort. (Occasionally a hymen is extra strong and may even need medical help, but this is rare.) If broken by force, and if the vagina is unlubricated then it will be painful. Relax *into* the pain, and divorce your mind if you can from what is happening. Fix your thoughts on something beautiful, or calming, remember back to your childhood Companion, and summon it to help you. Call Harriet and concentrate on her. Go away to a place you know that is full of peace and serenity. Try to go away inside your head and (this is most important) *pull the power of your virginity into yourself. If you do this you will empower yourself by the pain and the intention. The power will not be lost, nor will it go towards the rapist. He will not benefit from its breaking.*

To do this, imagine that your purity is a brilliant white dove that opens its wings and flies from your invaded body, up along the path of the spine, circling it in flight and flying straight into the very centre of your physical brain. Let the power explode there and fill you with that power. Drink it in and make it yours forever. It will not be easy, your mind and your thoughts will be drawn back to what is happening, but if you succeed even partially you will win a spiritual battle.

The Desecrated Grail

Rape is not just a crime of a physical and sexual nature, it is the spiritual assault of the sacred space of womanhood. I have said elsewhere (*First Steps in Ritual*) that if a man broke into a church and desecrated its altar he would be charged with a serious crime and the church itself would be cleansed and reconsecrated with all speed. The womb and the sacred way that leads to it, the vagina, and its locked door, the hymen, is the living church of womanhood. It is as much a place of worship as a chapel, cathedral, temple, druidic grove, or sacred circle. It is where Creation occurs, where Life is renewed.

Every male who enters that space should do so as an invited guest, he comes, as the old form of the marriage service says, 'with my body I thee worship'. The Great Mother has Her Temple of Life here and the woman is its high priestess, the living temple of life. Man enters, he makes a sacrifice of his own substance to the Goddess within and is blessed and renewed by Her and Her human priestess. He returns to the outer world refreshed and made whole. He has given and he has taken. He has *communed*. When the blessed and sanctified wafer is dropped into the blessed and sanctified chalice of wine, what we are seeing is a symbolic enactment of the coming together of the male and female elements to engender a Great Mystery. *This makes rape much more than a physical assault, it is the spiritual defilement of a sacred place, and it lays upon the perpetrator a karmic debt of enormous proportions.*

In a book written for women let me speak for a moment to men, all men. You are the seed bearer, woman is the seed carrier, both are sacred terms, sacred offices. Either of us may choose to mate or not, to create children or not as we wish, but for those who do so let me say this. The act of entering the body of another was designed to give pleasure as well as provide for the re-creation of ourselves in another human being. To defile that with violence debases the man far below the animal. There is no rape among our younger brethren, the female comes into season and opens her body willingly that her species may continue. Human women are raped and defiled every day in every country in the world. We can only suffer and fight back by means of a law weighted against us. YOU ARE THE ONES WHO CAN END IT. YOU ARE THE FATHERS, THE UNCLES, THE BROTHERS, THE SONS, WHO CAN SPEAK OUT AGAINST IT. YOU ARE, SOMETIMES, THOSE WHO COMMIT THE CRIME. We need your voices to help us, we need you, if there be a need, to seek help, we need your companionship, your support and your love, not your violence against our bodies.

The aftermath of rape can be devastating. Quite apart from the physical damage, there is the mental and emotional hurt to deal with for a long time afterwards. Use the power you withdrew from the 'breaking' to free you from the guilt and feeling of having been dirtied by the experience. Remember this if nothing else, *it was not your fault*. Leaving out the legal side of things, you will need to talk, to be counselled, to go through the experience with someone who is qualified to help you.

Once this is done you can be helped further. You can undergo a Reconsecration of the Womb. This is a ritual designed to cleanse, hallow, re-consecrate and anoint a woman who has gone through this experience, and others of a like nature.[1] It will be done for you by a woman qualified as a priestess, sometimes one who is also an ordained minister of the church. You will be surrounded by women who have shared the same kind of ordeal and who understand. It will release the final tension and inner pain so you can get on with your life. It is a simple, short ceremony that has an effect out of all proportion to its simplicity. It is now something that is done quite often and there are workshops held in many places now and in many countries where you can ask for this kind of help. [2]

Coming of Age

In Western Countries the age of consent, that is the age at which it is lawful for a person of either sex to have sexual intercourse, is usually sixteen, with the older age of twenty-one being considered true adulthood. You can get married at sixteen if you have the consent of your parents. Some European countries have a lower age of fifteen. At eighteen you no longer need parental consent.

The term 'coming of age' is all that is left of the Rites of Passage that once heralded the entering of the adult stage of life. In times past there were many such passage rites along the way. A boy was usually dressed in skirts until the age of five when he was 'breeched'. Some areas did it at three years. Then came the passage rite of puberty, and then marriage. There were times when a boy was considered old enough to go to war with his father, uncles and older brothers at the age of twelve. Powder monkeys on fighting ships in Nelson's day were often as young as eight or nine. Their passage into the adult world was often the loss of a limb, or even life itself.

Nowadays it is often a party and a new dress, a special present and all your friends around you. Sometimes you get a front door key and may now come and go as you please. But not quite. You have now passed through the door of womanhood, you must begin to *act* like a grown up as well. You get nothing for free, Daughter of Eve, things will be expected of you that previously were not expected of the child you used to be. This will include being responsible for things like doing your own laundry and ironing, helping with housework if you are still living at home, and realising it is getting close to the time when you will fly the nest and have a place of your own.

It is great fun and there is a feeling of being free for the first time. This euphoria lasts for about a month, especially if you have a place of your own. The moment when you get your very own phone bill is the moment when you realise what your parents have been going through for years. Trying to balance a bank statement, buying food without going bankrupt, not being able to 'borrow' your mother's new tights when your own have a run in them, all this is part of the Rites of Passage into the grown-up world.

Then there is the new feeling of loneliness. You will have to get used to coming back to an empty flat or apartment with no one to make you a cup of tea, have your dinner waiting, or listen to your day's story of woe. Welcome to the real world.

One last experience that you will, in your Maiden Years, undoubtedly undergo: you will lose a love. You may be rejected, you yourself may fall out of love, then again the object of your affections may never even glance your way. These things happen and when you are young they are devastating.

When you put as much emotion into something as a love affair, whether it is returned or not, it causes a very real interchange of energies. What is sometimes called an *arc thread* is formed from the subtle matter of the astral level and it fixes itself on to the loved one. This happens also when a sexual act takes place, even if it is a passing casual, one night stand (why do they call it that? One lies down most of the time!). With committed lovers, this simply increases the strength of their love for each other. However, when a relationship ends the threads are firmly implanted (which is why the modern version is seen as a Cupid's Dart or Arrow) and need to be extracted, or they will give rise to an emotional infection. Once the thread has withered the only emotion left will be of a gentle, 'Ah well, it was good while it lasted' kind. We have all seen what can happen when a love is not returned, or is cruelly rejected. The person is sick at heart and sometimes actually becomes physically ill.

Setting yourself free from such things is part and parcel of your female magic. Remember also that what you do for yourself you can also do for others. May I also remind you, Daughter of Eve, that it shows a caring and Goddess-orientated nature to withdraw your arc thread from the heart of another when your love for them has died. They may not have the knowledge to do it for themselves. You have, so the onus is on you to end it quickly and cleanly and set him free to love someone else. If it is you who has been rejected, remember you cannot order love to suit yourself. Love is part chemistry and part something we have yet to fully understand.

There is no need for you to go through torments of unrequited love, *although a little taste of it will not do you too much harm and all experience leads to wisdom.* You can get rid of those arc threads. Read on.

Notes

1 Write to Dolores Ashcroft-Nowicki,
   PO Box 215,
   St Helier,
   Jersey, CI.
2 Write to Arcania Courses,
   17 Union Passage,
   Bath BA1 1RE,
   for information on workshops held in Bath for this ceremony.

6

THE RITUALS

The First Flowing

This is a celebration for the 'newly arrived' young woman.
Gather her female friends around her, as many as possible,
in a large room, a small village hall, or out of doors if it's warm
enough. Simple food and drink should be available. Let
everyone be given the chance to bring something: fresh bread
rolls, butter, cheeses, cut meats, fruit, cake, biscuits, sausage
rolls. Done like this it is not expensive. Also it may be possible
for several girls to hold their First Flowing Rite together, for
it is very probable that many of them will begin their menses
on or about the same time.

This is *not* a party, it is a ritual along native lines but
incorporating certain other elements as well. First and
foremost, it is a thanksgiving that the girl(s) has reached this
important time in her life. Remember many children in the
world do not live past their fifth year. Secondly, it is a
thanksgiving to the Goddess for her Divine manifestation in
the girl(s) in the form of her newly declared womanhood.
Thirdly, it is an invocation to that Goddess for her future
health and prosperity.

Along with the food each person should bring along a
small gift, not for the celebrants, but with which to build an
altar of gifts that will on the morning after be given to a
charity, an orphanage, a hospital, or a home of some kind,
to be decided beforehand. These gifts are an expression
of thanks by friends and relatives for the lives and health of
the girls.

There should be a small altar or table against the Eastern

wall and on it a Chalice or large glass (it can be refilled when it is necessary), flowers, bowls of fruit, small almond-flavoured biscuits, (the almond is special to the goddess as it has the shape of the female genitals) and coloured candles. All on a white or red cloth. On either side on boxes or small tables covered with red crêpe paper build up the gifts. These can be food, wine, toiletries, biscuits, fruit, flowers, tinned goods, tea and preserves, things like pretty boxes of tissues, soaps, sweets and chocolate. The room should be lit with coloured lights or, so long as they are *safe*, coloured candles. A large chair is set before it, a small table to one side of it, and as many chairs as there are candidates on either side.

The oldest woman at the party acts as the Priestess. She should be ready to welcome each guest as they arrive, to take their gifts for the altar, and hand them on to helpers who will place them with all the others. The girls themselves should be hidden away, and not allowed to see the room or anything else pertaining to the celebrations. They might wear simple white robes that can be made from sheeting or even white rayon lining, and a small coronet of flowers and ribbons.

When everyone has arrived the oldest female member calls for silence. She then takes her place in the centre chair as the Crone. On the table at her side there is a tube of body paint, a saucer and a small stick or paint brush.

For each girl there is a gift, a silver chain with a small charm on it. The charm should be the same for all of them. The Chalice of wine and the almond cakes are put on the table as well. Before the Crone they spread a large white towel and on it a bowl or small baby bath one third full of warm water, big enough for the girl to stand in it with both feet, a jug of warm water scented with Ylang Ylang oil, and a large towel for each girl in a pile by the bowl. Three adult women are the helpers: two to hold up sheets to hide the girl as she is bathed (if they are not shy to stand naked in front of their women friends then dispense with these), and one to wrap her in towels and help her to dry off.

Now the music begins. Choose native rhythms that people can clap their hands to and stamp their feet (if doing this in a private house please warn neighbours). Didgeridoo music is also good.[1] Get them moving in a circle at first, clapping their hands to the music. It only needs one or two with a sense of rhythm to get the rest going. The idea is to build up a cone of power into which the girls will enter and at the centre of which the Crone will take them through their sacred cleansing, their marking on brow and breast and womb with the Crescent symbol of the Moon Goddess, their dressing in new clothes, or simply clean clothes, and their drinking of the wine and cakes of the Goddess.

Remember that the girls are waiting, they do not know what to expect, they are excited, a little apprehensive, and even a tiny bit scared of the new world that is opening up before them. Now the chanting can begin. This is done with one voice leading the rest. You may need to practise it a few times before the day, but it is a very simple tune with only three or four notes repeated all the time. The words are simply sonics that vibrate on a happy and slightly trance-inducing level. The sound of it will reach the girls in their room and heighten the effect on them.

The words and music of the chant are as shown below.

Keep the chant going with perhaps a different lead voice at each recommencement. Then someone goes to bring in the first girl. She is blindfolded before entering, then led around

the circle of chanting, hand-clapping women. She is stopped
the first time and given something either sharp, like pure
lemon juice, or slightly bitter, like tonic water, to drink. The
second time she is stopped she is given something sweet, like
a small amount of honey on her tongue. The third time she
is stopped she is slapped sharply on one hand and given a
gentle kiss on the other. Finally, she is brought before the
Crone (chanting stops).

Crone: (Girl's name), YOU HAVE COME TO THE GATE OF
WOMANHOOD, THE GATE OF THE MOON GODDESS TO
WHOM YOU ARE NOW BOUND MONTH BY MONTH.
THE BITTERNESS AND THE SWEETNESS ON YOUR
TONGUE IS TO REMIND YOU THAT LIFE HOLDS BOTH
BITTER AND SWEET MOMENTS. YOU MUST LEARN TO
COPE WITH BOTH OF THEM. THE SLAP AND THE KISS
REMIND YOU THAT SOMETIMES YOU WILL DO THINGS
WRONG AND HAVE TO PUT THEM RIGHT, AT OTHER
TIMES YOU WILL KNOW GREAT HAPPINESS AND JOY.
FOR BOTH YOU MUST GIVE THANKS. YOU WILL LEARN
WISDOM BY MAKING MISTAKES, AND GROW WITH THE
EXPERIENCE OF JOY. NOW YOU ENTER A NEW PHASE OF
YOUR LIFE, ONE THAT WILL BE WITH YOU FOR MANY,
MANY YEARS. IT IS NOT TO BE SEEN AS A CURSE OR AS
SOMETHING UNCLEAN, BUT AS THE TEMPLE OF YOUR
BODY WORKING TO THE PLAN. NOW IS THE MOMENT
TO LEAVE CHILDHOOD BEHIND.

The helpers hold up the sheets, and the third woman takes
off the robe and helps her to step into the bath. The Crone
comes and gently pours warm scented water over her
shoulders, allowing it to run down her body, back and front.
Then she steps out of the water and is dried and wrapped in
the towel. The blindfold is taken off. The Crone marks her on
the forehead and breast and over the womb in body paint with
the symbol of the crescent moon.
    She is now dressed in her new underwear and dress and
either shoes or slippers. While this takes places the Crone
returns to her place and the girl is brought before her and
kneels. The Crone places her hands on her head and blesses
her in her own words. Then she gives her wine from the cup

to drink and a small piece of almond cake. The girl is given her candle, lit from the altar candle, and she goes to sit on her chair. The water is taken out, fresh brought in and the next girl is called. The chanting begins again, and the short ceremony is gone through a second time. When all have gone through they are called before the Crone to kneel and listen.

Crone: CHILDREN NO LONGER, YOU ARE WOMEN TRUE, CLEANSED BY THE WATER WHICH IS RULED BY THE MOON, HAVING TASTED THE BITTER AND THE SWEET, KNOWN HARSHNESS AND TENDERNESS. KNOW THAT THE GODDESS IS ALWAYS WITH YOU AND WITHIN YOU. WHEN THE MOON SUMMONS THE BLOOD FROM YOUR BODY, IT IS OBEYING HER CALL. SEE IT AS AN OFFERING TO HER. TAKE NOW FROM MY HAND THE GIFTS OF YOUR FAMILY. (places a silver charm around the neck of each girl) THESE MARK YOU AS HAVING BEEN TOUCHED AND ACCEPTED BY THE GODDESS.

A helper brings the Chalice and each girl in turn douses her candle in it. It is then taken round for each person to sip from (grape juice can be used instead of wine, and the odd bit of candle wax will not harm you).

Now the girls become the Hostesses and take round the food and drink and the party can begin. It is customary where possible to choose a tree in a wooded area and once or twice a year to bury the first day's menstruation cloths at its roots fairly deeply. The blood will feed the tree and bring about a kinship between you. It will give you comfort and energy when you need it. Just lean against it, call it sister and ask for help. The great earth energy used by the tree will flow into you and sustain you.

The Coming of Age
This could be done a few days before any ordinary 18th or 21st birthday party, or if all the participants are of a like mind and belief then it can become a part of the proceedings. (This particular ritual can of course be adapted for a young man.) I have taken the basic idea from the Scottish 'First Footing' rite used at the New Year, but added to it is the form of a Leaving and Returning Rite.

You will need the following: a small table in the main room set up in the style of an altar with a white cloth and a centre light. Beside it on the right side place a small bag, something about the size of a flight bag, no bigger, on the left side place a new pair of shoes for the person coming of age. On the altar itself put a photograph of the family all together, a small fresh bread roll (or, if possible, a small homemade loaf), a piece of cheese, some salt, a white Rose, a pound coin, piece of coal and a sharp knife. You will also need an unlit white candle in a holder, and if possible a lantern – the kind that holds a candle inside is best, but if not then an oil lantern. If nothing else is to hand then use a good powerful torch. Lastly, a small tray with a glass for everyone and a bottle of wine, or even something like Drambuie or Brandy if you wish.

What you are enacting in this Rite is the Tarot card of The Fool. Gather everyone together with the Mother at the altar. The new adult wears about her waist a scarlet cord.

Mother: (lights the altar light) EIGHTEEN (or TWENTY-ONE) YEARS AGO YOU, (young woman's name), CAME INTO THIS WORLD AND INTO THIS FAMILY. WE HAVE SEEN YOU GROW FROM BABYHOOD TO CHILDHOOD, TO GIRLHOOD AND NOW YOU ARE A WOMAN AND AN ADULT. THE TIME HAS COME FOR YOU TO BE INDEPENDENT, FREE FROM THE FAMILY AND THE PARENTS WHO BROUGHT YOU TO BIRTH. IT IS TIME TO SPREAD YOUR WINGS, MAKE YOUR OWN MISTAKES AND FIND YOUR OWN WAY IN THE WORLD. WHEN YOU WERE BORN YOU WERE CONNECTED TO ME BY AN UMBILICAL CORD. THIS HAS BOUND US TOGETHER THROUGHOUT YOUR TIME OF GROWING. NOW I FREE YOU. (cuts the scarlet cord with the knife) NOW WE ARE BOUND ONLY BY OUR LOVE AND RESPECT FOR EACH OTHER, NOT ONLY AS MOTHER AND DAUGHTER BUT AS WOMAN AND WOMAN.

Father: WHEN YOU WERE SMALL I WAS YOUR PROTECTOR, NOW YOUR PATH WILL BECOME SEPARATE FROM MINE. THERE WILL BE TIMES WHEN I AM NOT NEAR ENOUGH TO PROTECT YOU, YOU MUST LEARN TO FIGHT FOR YOURSELF. NOW YOU ARE A WOMAN AND ONE DAY IT MAY BE THAT YOU WILL HAVE NEED AGAIN

OF YOUR FATHER'S LOVE AND PROTECTION. IT WILL BE THERE FOR YOU ALWAYS. WHEN YOU WERE SMALL I AND YOUR MOTHER FED AND CLOTHED YOU. NOW YOU WILL BE DOING THESE THINGS FOR YOURSELF. BUT ON THIS SPECIAL NIGHT, FOR THE LAST TIME I SEND YOU OUT INTO THE WORLD WITH A GIFT. SHOES TO WALK THE ROUGH ROADS OF LIFE. (puts shoes on her feet) MAY YOU TRAVEL LIGHTLY AND SWIFTLY, WITH GOOD COMPANIONS AND A JOYFUL HEART, AND RETURN TO US OFTEN AND WITH LOVE.

Grandparent: IN YOU I SEE MY LINE GOING ON INTO THE FUTURE, I AM CONTENT THAT THIS IS SO. I HAVE SEEN MANY CHANGES, MOST OF THEM FROM THE TIME THAT YOU WERE BORN. I PRAY THAT YOU WILL FIND LOVE AND HAPPINESS IN THE YEARS AHEAD, AND THAT YOU WILL SEE YOUR OWN GRANDCHILDREN START ON THE JOURNEY THAT YOU NOW TAKE. MY GIFT TO YOU IS THIS TRAVELLING BAG, AND IN IT I WILL PLACE THIS PHOTOGRAPH, AS A MEMORY OF THIS NIGHT AND OF THE FAMILY THAT WILL ALWAYS BE HERE FOR YOU. (places photo in bag and gives it to the young woman) I HAVE TRAVELLED THE ROAD YOU NOW TAKE, AND I KNOW WHAT MAY LIE AHEAD OF YOU. I GIVE YOU THREE THINGS TO TAKE WITH YOU. BREAD, THE HOLY FOOD, MADE FROM THE CORN'S SACRIFICE. (breaks loaf in two and puts half into the bag) SALT, WITHOUT WHICH WE CANNOT LIVE. (puts salt into bag) AND CHEESE, THE GIFT GIVEN TO US BY THE ANIMAL KINGDOM. (puts cheese into bag) WALK IN SAFETY.

Relative: MY GIFT IS THE GIFT OF A COIN, A SYMBOL OF PROSPERITY TO COME. BUT NEVER FORGET TO GIVE AS WELL AS TO RECEIVE. NEVER TURN AWAY FROM THOSE IN NEED, NEVER LOOK UPON WEALTH AS THE ULTIMATE IN LIFE. (puts coin in bag)·

Friend: MY GIFT IS THIS PIECE OF COAL, A SYMBOL OF WARMTH AND SHELTER. MAY YOUR HOUSE NEVER BE COLD, NEVER BE WITHOUT FIRE OR COMFORT. ALWAYS MAKE ROOM BY THE FIRE FOR SOMEONE WHO HAS NEED. IN THIS WAY YOU WILL ALWAYS BE BLESSED. (puts coal in bag)

Mother: I HAVE A LAST GIFT TO YOU, SOMETHING TO REMIND YOU OF HOME AND OF US. THIS WHITE ROSE, THE SYMBOL OF LOVE, LOVE WITHOUT THOUGHT OF SELF AND THEREFORE THE SYMBOL OF A MOTHER'S LOVE. (gives rose)

Father: I TOO HAVE A LAST GIFT. IT IS THE KEY TO THIS HOUSE. IN TIME TO COME YOU WILL HAVE MANY KEYS, AND MAYBE MANY HOUSES OF YOUR OWN. BUT THIS KEY IS SPECIAL BECAUSE IT SETS YOU FREE, WHILE ALLOWING YOU TO RETURN AS YOU WILL. (gives key)

Mother: LET US GATHER ROUND AND SHARE THE BREAD AND THE WINE TOGETHER. (father breaks the bread and salts it, and hands it round. The Mother offers round the glasses) A BLESSING ON US ALL AND ON YOU, (young woman's name), AS YOU TAKE THE ROAD OF LIFE.

All eat and drink together.

Father: NOW YOU MUST GO.

Coat and outdoor clothing brought and put on.

Mother: TAKE THIS LANTERN TO LIGHT YOUR WAY. I WILL SET THE CANDLE IN THE WINDOW TO LIGHT YOUR WAY BACK AGAIN. (sets lighted candle in window)

Everyone takes the new adult to the door and watches her go, waving and calling. It is important that she actually goes somewhere that takes a little time. If it is possible, she should spend at least an hour away. Then she returns. In the meantime a table has been laid and made ready. Everyone waits until they hear the knock on the door, and the key in the latch. Then is the time to welcome back the traveller and to set another place at the table.

The young woman is now a full adult and may come and go as she pleases, though she still has to learn responsibility.

Loosing the Kestos

This ritual is really only for those who have their lives fully bound up with the mysteries; for those young women who have followed the path of the virgin priestess and kept their gift until the right moment. This does not always, in our modern times, happen at the time of the marriage. It can happen before then and since free will has been given to all this is a matter for those concerned and not for others to decry.

This then is a ritual that precedes the loosing of the Kestos. Therefore I suppose it can be counted as a sexual ritual. It has a secondary title, 'The Bestowal of the Gift'. First, as always, I will ask you to be sure of what you are doing for this is not something to be given lightly. If you are sure, then follow the old way of the Priestesses of Naradek.

This is in many ways an initiation into a new path of womanhood. It will hold both joy and pain. After the gift has been given you will never be the same person. Therefore, as before all initiations you should keep a *vigil*. Nowadays the giving often occurs without thought or planning, as the result of a party and too much alcohol and too little self control. The beauty of the moment is therefore lost, buried beneath the headache and nausea of the morning after. What should be a unique, wonderful and fulfilling time in your life, becomes a blur of half-remembered fumblings, and the fear of expecting to be discovered any moment.

You plan your birthday parties, your engagements parties, your wedding, and this is just as important. It should not be one-sided, both should be aware of what is happening and why. Both should pay their physical temples the compliment of being in their full awareness.

The vigil should be kept in a place of quietness and beauty. It need not be the night before, it is up to you. It is simply to allow you time in which to reflect on your life until now, the way in which it will change after the Kestos has been loosened. You are a woman legally of age, you can vote, you can drive a car, but with the giving of the Gift, you will come entirely into your own Feminine Power. Think about the person to whom you are giving this Gift and the empowerment that will come to him. By the same token the one who will receive it should also take time to be quiet and contemplate the meaning of the untying of the Kestos, think of it in the sense of being the Girdle of Aphrodite, the Goddess of Love. If you are of the same beliefs and traditions of your lover, then you will understand when I say that the love that sustains the giving should on that first occasion be offered to the Goddess Herself. If this is done then She will grant you both Her favour and Her blessing for as long as you are together.

In the mountains and valleys of what used to be Russian

Georgia there was a wedding tradition that has long since died out. The bride would be laced into a leather corselet under her wedding clothes, which fastened down the front with sometimes as many as one hundred knots. If the bride had been the victim of an arranged marriage and was not happy about her parents' choice of groom, she would wet the knots and the leather would shrink. Custom forbade the groom to use his knife, so he had to undo each and every knot before claiming his bride.

I think one hundred leather knots would be pushing your lover's patience a little too far, but certainly the making of a Kestos would not be beyond the ability of either the girl or one of her friends. It may be as simple or as elaborate as you like to make it (see illustration). It may be made of any material, though silk is traditional. Its decoration may be the tiniest of beads in an intricate pattern, or silk thread embroidery. Tiny bells along the edge in ancient times made the belt very difficult to get off without warning the Mistress of Novices. In those days the belts were usually fastened with intricate knots and difficult to take off. Chastity belts came into Europe when the Crusaders saw similar things in the East, and with their twisted minds set about making their own version . . .in metal. The modern version of the Kestos is the decorative hip belt of the Belly Dancer.

Cut two sides of main material and two of iron vilene. Sew the iron vilene to the main material as a lining. Embroider the belt to taste and add a fringe. Make eyelet holes and add lacings. Large sequins, beads or coins may be added.

The belt is not a symbol of slavery to the male, it is a symbol of freedom of choice. The choice of the woman to give her Gift of Innocence to whomsoever she wishes. By allowing the man of her choice to undo the lacings she is affirming that freedom.

Once made, the Kestos may be put away until the time comes for it to be used. It may even be worn beneath your wedding dress, for until it is untied, you are still *your own woman*. It may be that you wish this to be a simple action without words or, if you so wish, a proper ritual may be made.

You will need the following: a small altar laid with a white cloth, and lit with rose-scented candles; a small statue of a Goddess figure before which burns a little Venus incense or, if you cannot use incense, then spray a little perfume into the

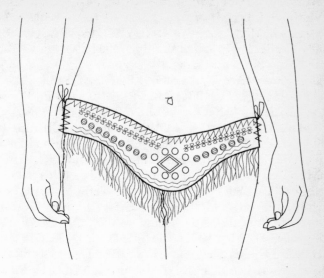

air; white and deep pink flowers, preferably Roses; a centre light; a cup of wine; an apple; salt and water that have both been blessed and mixed together.

The two people concerned kneel before the altar and the invocation to Aphrodite is made:

Both: GRACIOUS AND MOST LOVELY GODDESS, LOOK UPON THE MAN AND THE WOMAN WHO KNEEL BEFORE YOU. WE CALL UPON YOU IN THE ANCIENT WAY, WITH PERFUME, WITH FLOWERS, WITH WINE AND WITH THE SYMBOL OF THE WISDOM OF WOMAN.

Woman: I AM WOMAN, I ACKNOWLEDGE MYSELF TO BE A DAUGHTER OF THE GODDESS. I AM FREE TO MAKE MY OWN CHOICE IN THE WAYS OF LOVE. I AM READY TO MAKE THE GIFT THAT MAY BE GIVEN ONLY ONCE. WITH THAT GIFT I WILL LOVINGLY AND KNOWINGLY EMPOWER THE MAN AT MY SIDE. AT THAT MOMENT GREAT GODDESS, ENTER INTO HIS HEART THAT HE MAY KNOW YOU IN ALL THE FEMININE GLORY THAT IS YOURS AND YOURS ALONE. IN THE GIVING MAY I

GROW TO BE GREATER THAN I AM NOW. LET MY POWER FLOW THROUGH ME TO THE ENHANCEMENT OF MYSELF AS A WOMAN AND AS A HUMAN BEING, AND TO THE HUMAN RACE AS A WHOLE. TEACH ME TO KNOW MYSELF, THAT I MAY FIND WITHIN THE WOMAN I CAN BE.

Man: I AM MAN. I ACKNOWLEDGE MYSELF TO BE A SON OF THE GOD. I TOO AM FREE TO MAKE MY OWN CHOICE AND I CHOOSE TO BE WITH THE WOMAN AT MY SIDE. I KNOW THE POWER OF THE GIFT SHE IS OFFERING AND I HONOUR HER, AND THE GODDESS WHO DWELLS WITHIN HER, FOR ITS GIVING. AT THE MOMENT OF MY ACCEPTANCE OF THE GIFT I OFFER MYSELF TO THE GODDESS IN THE POWER AND MAJESTY OF THAT MOMENT THAT WILL NEVER COME AGAIN. COME TO ME THEN LADY OF LOVE AND BEAUTY THAT I MAY KNOW THEE FULLY IN THE PERSON AND BODY OF MY CHOSEN. I ACCEPT THE POWER AND ASK FOR GUIDANCE IN ITS USING. TEACH ME TO KNOW MYSELF, THAT I MAY BECOME THE MAN I WAS MEANT TO BE.

Woman takes the salt and water and sprinkles the bed with it.

Woman: WITH HALLOWED SALT AND BLESSED WATER I CLEANSE THE PLACE OF OUR SLEEPING.

Man takes the roses and scatters the petals over the bed.

Man: WITH THESE FLOWERS I WILL PREPARE A COUCH FOR THE GODDESS WITHIN YOU.

Woman censes the bed with incense or perfume.

Woman: WITH SCENTED SMOKE I MAKE SACRED THE COUCH OF MY LOVE.

She brings the wine to her lover and offers it to him.

DRINK WINE WITH ME MY LOVE THAT THE COMMUNION BETWEEN US MAY BE MADE BINDING.

They share the cup, and then she brings the apple.

ONCE MORE I, WOMAN, OFFER THE APPLE OF KNOWLEDGE TO THEE, MAN. DO NOT FEAR TO EAT OF IT, FOR ITS SWEETNESS HOLDS THE SECRET OF LIFE.

He takes a bite and then she does the same. Now they take off any clothing they may be wearing. All that the woman now wears is the sacred Kestos.

Woman: I, (woman's name), GIVE THEE, (man's name), LEAVE TO LOOSEN THE SACRED KESTOS OF MY INNOCENCE. TO THEE I SHALL BE THE GODDESS, TO ME THOU SHALT BE THE HORNED GOD AND TOGETHER WE SHALL BE DIVINE.

The Man loosens and takes off the Kestos and lays it aside. The Rite continues as the Goddess shall will it.

The Ritual of Reconsecration

There is a tendency when one speaks of laying a woman upon an altar for the inexperienced and the misinformed to scream 'Black Magic' at the top of their voices. But all things destined to be used for the celebration of the Mysteries, Christian or Pagan, are consecrated upon an altar. Is a woman and the holy place within her less worthy?

You will need a couch or a table long enough to take the full length of the woman to be healed; cover it with a white cloth. Have a small table, also covered with a white cloth, some three feet in front of it to act as an altar; on it, place containers of salt, water and sweet oil, some burning incense, and a chalice a quarter full of wine. You will also require a bowl of mixed water and wine and two clean cloths. Two women act as sponsors, the others as witnesses. The woman herself should be dressed in a robe or loose garment, her feet bare, and she and her sponsors stand outside the circle or sacred place. Inside are the other women and the priestess.

Priestess: WHO WILL SPONSOR THIS WOMAN TO BE HEALED?

The sponsors must answer and come forward. They take the bowl of water and wine and the cloths. They lay down a cloth for her to stand on and then wash the woman's hands and feet with wine and water, and dry them with the other cloth.

Priestess: IS IT YOUR WILL AND YOUR DESIRE TO BE HEALED AND MADE WHOLE?

Woman: IT IS MY WILL AND DESIRE.

Priestess: (to sponsors) BRING HER TO THE ALTAR AND LAY HER DOWN.

The sponsors lift the woman over the circle and carry her to the altar and lay her down on it. Thus her cleansed feet never touch the earth. The two sponsors stand at her head and feet supporting them gently so that she is symbolically suspended between Heaven and Earth.

Priestess: (facing East, arms outstretched) APOLLO, LORD OF THE HEALING HAND, SUN CHILD, VICTOR OF DELPHI, I CALL THEE TO THE EAST IN THE FORM OF THE RISING SUN. WE HAVE NEED OF THEE.

(facing South) ASCLEPIUS, SON OF THE SUN, GUARDIAN OF THE SOLAR SERPENT, I CALL THEE TO THE SOUTH IN THE FORM OF THE SUN AT NOON. WE HAVE NEED OF THEE.

(facing West) HYGEIA, PRIESTESS OF THE TEMPLE OF THE BODY, I CALL THEE TO THE WEST IN THE FORM OF THE WATERS OF LIFE AND ENERGY.

(facing North) PANACEA, PRIESTESS OF THE TEMPLE OF THE QUIET MIND, I CALL THEE TO THE NORTH IN THE FORM OF THE DOVE OF INNER PEACE.

She takes up the incense and goes round to stand over the woman (see plan), and passes the burning incense up and down her body.

WITH BURNING HERBS I CLEANSE THEE, WITH SWEET SMELLING INCENSE I DRIVE PAIN AND HURT FROM THEE. WITH SCENTED SMOKE I HALLOW THEE.

The Priestess returns to the altar, as always moving sunwise, to make a circle. She takes the salt and water, cleanses them and tips salt into the water. She then takes the salt and water and goes as before to stand by the woman. Tipping the liquid in small quantities into her hand, she bathes the face and sprinkles the body and feet.

WITH SWEET WATER I CLEANSE THEE AND WASH AWAY THE TEARS OF PAIN AND SORROW. WITH SALT I CLEANSE THEE AND MAKE THEE PURE AND SACRED ONCE MORE.

The Priestess returns to the altar, takes up the chalice, goes to the woman and moistens her lips with wine. Then she lifts up the chalice and invokes the Great Female Principle of the Universe.

THOU WHO ARE EVER CHASTE AND VIRGIN, THE MOTHER OF ALL LIVING, RENEW AND RECONSECRATE THE SACRED CENTRE OF THIS WOMAN. MAKE HER CLEAN AND CHASTE ONCE MORE. MAKE HER

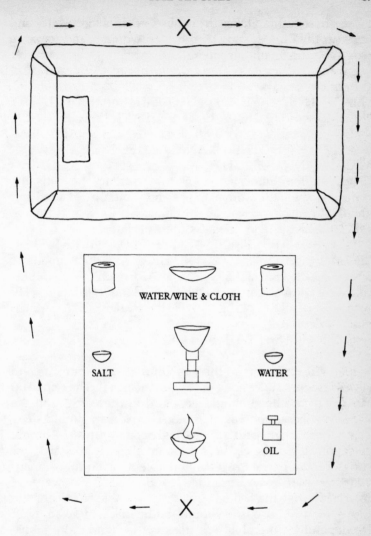

WATER/WINE & CLOTH

SALT   WATER

OIL

CONSCIOUS OF HER WOMANHOOD AS SOMETHING
OF BEAUTY AND HOLINESS. RETURN TO HER, HER
IMAGE OF HERSELF, AS A CHILD, MAID, WOMAN AND
WISE ONE. (as she speaks, she brings the chalice down
slowly until it rests upon the womb) WHAT IS FILLED WITH
LIGHT ABOVE SHALL BE FILLED WITH LIGHT BELOW.
WHAT IS PERFECT IN THE UPPER REALMS SHALL BE
MADE PERFECT IN THE LOWER.

The priestess then takes the chalice, returns to the altar and picks up the oil, goes to stand by the woman, and makes a circle with the oil on her forehead, between her breasts, over her womb, on her palms, and under her feet. As each place is marked she says:

MADE HOLY ARE THY THOUGHTS AND ALL THY DREAMS, MADE HOLY IS THE HEART WITHIN THEE, MADE HOLY IS THY WOMB. THY HANDS SHALL HEAL THE HURTS OF OTHERS, AND THY FEET SHALL WALK FOREVER IN THE LIGHT.

The Priestess returns the oil to the altar and bids the sponsors to help the woman to rise and stand up, unaided and whole. She gives the woman the chalice so she may drink the rest of the wine. The Priestess then declares:

YE WHO ARE PRESENT, BEHOLD YOUR SISTER, RENEWED IN BODY, SOUL AND HEART. (to the woman she says:) NEVER DOUBT THAT YOU ARE NOW CLEANSED AND MADE WHOLE AND HOLY. GO OUT INTO THE WORLD AND WALK WITH PRIDE IN YOUR WOMANHOOD.

All: SO MOTE IT BE THIS DAY.

A small gift of flowers to the woman from her sponsors and witnesses will make a good ending to the ritual. The wine and water from the bowl should be given to the earth, and the cloths washed as soon as possible. The woman should sleep early on that night and eat sparingly for the next 24 hours.

If, and this is a big IF, there is a man either in the family or who is known to the Priestess and acceptable to the woman, a further part may be added to the ritual. However, I emphasize that the woman may not be able to accept the suggestion and, if so, she should not be made to do so. A lot will depend on the ability of the man to handle the whole thing with delicacy and tact.

At the end of the ritual, the woman is asked by the Priestess if she feels ready to forgive the man responsible. If she says not, then let it be. If she says yes, then the following may be added to the rite.

One of the sponsors goes to bring the man, who stands as a symbol of the Male Principle. He is brought to the altar before the woman and kneels.

Man: (takes her hands in his) THOU ART WOMAN, THOU ART HOLY, THOU ART THE CHALICE. FOR WHAT HAS BEEN DONE TO THEE BY MAN, I, AS MAN SYMBOLIC, ASK THY FORGIVENESS. I OFFER TO THEE THE HAND OF MAN IN LOVE, IN FRIENDSHIP, AND IN RESPECT. WILL YOU, AS WOMAN BETRAYED, ACCEPT ME AS YOUR FRIEND?

Woman: I WILL ACCEPT THEE.

Man: LET THERE BE PEACE AND LOVE BETWEEN US AND IN TOKEN OF THIS I OFFER THE KISS OF PEACE. (rises and kisses her hand and her brow) THOU ART WOMAN, THOU ART BLESSED, THOU ART MADE SACRED BY THIS RITE. AS MAN SYMBOLIC, I ACKNOWLEDGE THIS. GIVE ME, I PRAY, THY LEAVE TO DEPART IN PEACE.

Woman: DEPART, AND PEACE BE BETWEEN THEE AND ME.

The man leaves, and the ritual ends in the same way as above.

Extracting Cupid's Dart

A considerable part of 'magic' deals with correspondences, that is, the idea that things that look alike, sound alike, act alike, somehow or other interact with each other. For instance, when you have a chill and a feverish cold you shake and quiver. A willow tree also shakes and quivers . . .and its bark was once used to make a rather revolting drink and given to people suffering from the Ague as it was called then. It worked then, it would work now if we didn't have a synthetic, easy-to-take substance that duplicates what was in that willow bark tea . . .namely aspirin. Getting rid of arc threads is rather similar. We use something that looks, feels, and acts in the same way as the 'love arrow'.

First, let us look at the procedure for loosing yourself from another person, but let me warn you that you must play your part and not put yourself into a position where new threads can get to you again. *Also remember that in freeing yourself you will also help to free the other person, leaving you both free to seek other loves.* I say this because one of the methods used here is a very old one and at first glance looks dubious. I assure you there is no need to worry, as my own unreserved dedication, my initiate's oath to the Light, does not allow me to lead you astray. To do so would incur a retribution I do not like to think about.

Let us look at the scenario: You and another person have been romantically involved for some time, therefore the threads are deeply embedded. You no longer wish to continue the relationship. Maybe neither of you wish this, in which case it is a lot easier – you may even persuade him to work with you.

You will need a length of red thread, ordinary cotton, two brand new needles, a pair of sharp scissors and, if your former love is not there, a photograph of him. Let me explain all these strange requirements. The red thread represents the arc thread, red because that is the colour of love and passion. The needles symbolise the 'Cupid's darts' which must be removed. The scissors cut the threads up after they have been removed. The photo is to represent your lover. *Please* return to him this photo and *all* photos you have of him or of the two of you together and ask him to tear them up. In this way you leave nothing on which a spark can be blown into life again.

You need to work at midnight. Why? Because that is the point when time is between the worlds of old night and new day. If you have everything ready you can complete the whole ritual within the time it takes for the clock to sound twelve strikes. In this way you work it all within 'no time' and the power is confined to within that space. Your former lover will be fast asleep and will not feel a thing. First, begin as with all ritual work, with a cleansing of your place of working. We do this by means of the Rose Cross Ritual, this may be used to prepare for any ritual you do.

Start thus:

Stand in the centre, go to the South-East Corner and make a large Calvary Cross. (This is the usual Christian Cross with a longer downward-pointing bar and a shorter bar two thirds of the way up.) Then, with your finger, make a circle in the air and, pointing to the centre of it, vibrate the Name Yeheshua. This name is a Rosicrucian compilation of the God-Name *Yod-Heh-vau-Heh* with the letter 'Shin', representing the human spirit, impacted into it. Draw the circle quite rapidly, as if you were setting a top spinning to form a vortex of force oriented by the Cross. On sounding the Name the figure can be seen to solidify from an outline of light to an actual blood-red rose blooming on a gold cross.

With arm outstretched before you, go to the South-West and repeat, then to the North-west and repeat, and then to the North-East and repeat. Complete your circumambulation by returning to the South-East, pointing at the centre of the original Rose-Cross. In the course of this circumambulation visualise your finger tracing a line of light. Return to the centre, raising your arm to trace a vertical arc of Light, and trace the Rose-Cross above your head and vibrate the Name. Go to the North-West and bring down your hand to point at the centre of the Rose-Cross there. There is no need to retrace it or recall the name.

Turn right about to face the South-East and retrace your steps, but now tracing an arc of light through the floor to make a Rose-Cross under your feet in the centre. Vibrate the Name. Complete tracing the vertical circle by returning to South-East and bringing your arm up to point at the Rose-Cross already there.

Raising your arm, return to centre, picking up the Rose-

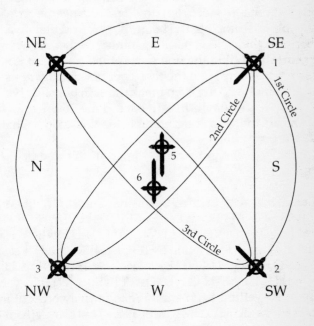

Cross above your head. Vibrate the Name to mark the start of the third circle, although there is no need to retrace the Rose-Cross. Trace the circle down to the North-East. No need to retrace the Rose-Cross there, or to vibrate the Name again.

Trace the cross and the circle under the floor to link up with the Rose-Cross beneath your feet in the centre.

Trace the circle up to the South-West Rose-Cross. Complete the circle by returning to the centre, bringing your arm up to the Rose-Cross above your head there.

Lower your arm and make a Rose-Cross of yourself by performing the Qabalistic Cross. To do this you should touch the forehead and say ATEH, point down to the floor and say MALKUTH, touch the right shoulder and say VE GEVURAH, touch the left shoulder and say VE GEDULAH, bring the hands together over the heart and say LE OLAM AMEN. Now strongly visualise yourself as the centre of the network of Rose-Crosses around, above and below you.

Practise that ritual until you know it by heart, it is an invaluable cleansing and protecting ritual. Now you are ready to begin. On a small table you should have gathered everything you need. Thread both needles with a single piece of cotton about four feet in length. Place one needle *very lightly* into the photo – not into the heart, but around that area. I say again, *very lightly*. Now, place the other needle just over your own heart, by sliding the fine point of the needle (if it is new it will be very sharp) into the first layer of skin. If you use just the very point it will not even break the skin but slide between the layers of the epidermis (I have done it on myself). It will cling to the skin long enough for you to do what you have to do.

Take the scissors and cut the thread in the middle, saying as you do so:

I, (your name), DO SET YOU, (his name), FREE FROM ALL BINDINGS OF AFFECTION, AS I SET MYSELF FREE FROM THE SAME BINDINGS. I LEAVE YOU WITH GRATITUDE FOR WHAT WE HAVE HAD TOGETHER, AND WITH A BLESSING FOR YOUR FUTURE LIFE. I WISH YOU A LONG LIFE WITH HEALTH AND HAPPINESS WITH A NEW LOVE WHO WILL BE TO YOU WHAT I CAN NO LONGER BE. I ASK YOU TO SET ME FREE WITH THE SAME

BLESSING. IN THE NAME OF THE LORDS OF LIGHT, I CUT THE TIES BETWEEN US.

Now pull out the needle from the photo.

THE ARC THREAD IS CUT, THE ARROW HAS BEEN REMOVED, BE BLESSED IN ALL YOU DO FROM NOW ON.

Pull the needle from your own body.

THE ARC THREAD HAS BEEN CUT, THE ARROW HAS BEEN REMOVED, MAY I BE BLESSED IN MY FUTURE LIFE AND LOVING.

Now gather up the thread and the needles and wrap them in a clean handkerchief. This must be buried in the earth within a few minutes of the ritual. If necessary some earth in a pot will do, but then it must be taken and reburied in the ground as soon as possible. The photo must, as I have said, be buried or otherwise disposed of, and the rest returned. If this is not possible then tie them all together and bury them as well, but make sure it is deep so they will rot quickly into the earth. Both of you are now free to find happiness with someone else.

Notes

1   *Thunderdrums* Scott Fitzgerald.
Nature Recordings,
PO Box 2749,
Friday Harbour,
WA 98250.

Songs of the Spirit Lisa Thiel.
Sacred Dream Productions,
PO Box 931 424,
LA, Cal 90093.

Songs of the Red Man Vols 1 and 2 John Richardson.
New World Cassettes,
PO Box 15,
Twickenham,
TW1 4SP.

All available from Arcania,
17 Union Passage,
Bath BA1 1RE.

PART 3
HIGH SUMMER
Fulfilment

7

THE BRIDE
AND THE MOTHER

In this chapter we will look at the traditional roles of Wife and Mother. They are roles which have changed out of all recognition since our grandmothers' day. Now a Wife is not just someone who cooks and cleans and looks after her children, she is a person in her own right. She may have a job, or maybe even run her own business. She will expect her husband to understand her needs for fulfilment outside the home as well as inside it. She will expect their marriage to be a partnership with all that it implies.

As a Mother she will want to provide her children with the best life and education she can. There are some women for whom the home and the family are, and always will be enough, others who will happily place their talents on hold until their children are older or have left home, still others will seek to combine both worlds.

There can never be just one way, it must always be the decision of a woman and her husband, lover or partner. No one else knows what is right for that particular family. There are some women who have no desire for children or, for that matter, for anything more than an occasional partner in their lives. Their lives are bound up in a career which fulfils her needs. We will deal with the 'Warrior Maid', in the next chapter.

Marriage

For those who do want a home and a family, marriage is usually the way they choose. The wedding day therefore becomes a genuine Rite of Passage, a moment when one moves from one part of life to another. It holds different responsibilities and viewpoints, you will have to get used to giving and taking instead of pleasing only yourself.

Marriage is a sacrament, one of the Great Mysteries, and it should always be taken to heart, its meaning both on the inner levels and in the physical world meditated upon and understood. It is much more than a chance to dress up in special clothes and give a big party. It is, Daughter of Eve, a time of great change, a time for the final growing-up of the child you once were. Before you lies a new life, perhaps in more than one meaning of those words.

You will leave your own home or that of your parents and make a home with another person. You may think you know that person very well, but no one knows another until they have lived intimately with them for a while . . . sometimes not even then!

There are some areas of the wedding service you may, if you are a modern young woman, have trouble with. The first one is when the Priest asks 'Who giveth this woman to this man?' I have heard many squawks of indignation from women about this, ranging from the indignant 'I am not a parcel to be handed over from one man to another', to 'I belong to myself so I should be able to speak for myself'. If I might just have a few words here.

When, in years to come, your own daughter stands at the altar to be married, you will no doubt shed a few tears. Sneak a close look at your husband. He may not admit to it, but he will feel like crying as well. You see men are not always the lying, cheating, lazy, no good !@$#%*&$@!'s that some would have us believe. There are men out there who are good, kind, gentle and loving. Your husband, like you, will be at that moment saying goodbye to his baby girl, just as your father at your wedding. Your father has looked after you, cherished you, spanked you, yelled at you and loved you for a long time. He feels responsible for your well-being and happiness. Suddenly another man has appeared and takes away the bigger part of your affections. He will *never* admit to it, but this can be devastating to a 'Dad'.

By allowing him to 'hand you over', by letting him place your hand in that of another man, who will take his little girl away from him, you are giving your father a chance to cut an arc thread of a slightly different nature to the others we have talked about. If you say to him 'I want to do this myself', you are in fact saying, 'I deny that you have ever had a responsibility for me, or taken care of me, it has no meaning for me'. Allow him to let you go in a traditional way.

Next sticking point, the word 'obey'. Well, this is one you have to decide for yourself. If your husband-to-be is getting hot under the collar with this one, there are a couple of alternatives: the first is to suggest new wording – you could say '. . . to love, honour and acknowledge', for example; the second is to say it, but cross your fingers under your wedding bouquet!

Not always fully understood (and, in my personal view, it was a bad mistake to change it) is that lovely phrase, 'with my body I thee worship'. The modernised version of the wedding ceremony is, to my mind, an abomination. I whole-heartedly loathe the New Version of Church Services. I much prefer the old language which had a ring of truth and beauty about it. For a man to say, 'all my worldly goods with thee I share' is a farce, since ten to one he, or she, has stipulated a nuptial agreement before the wedding anyway. When a man says, before an altar, 'with my body I thee worship', he is paying homage to the Goddess that lives within every woman in the ancient way, sexually and with love. To worship someone or something is to venerate it. (Of course, gentlemen, you might slightly reword it at the time, *accidentally you understand*, to 'with my body I *give* thee honour'.)

There is no need for me to write a special ritual for a wedding day. That traditional, beautiful service is of itself a rite no one can improve upon. What I would suggest is that the two of you sit down quietly some weeks before the wedding and read over the words of the service. It really does not matter if the faith is not yours, it is a solemn pact between two people to love and support each other. Read beneath the words and seek out the old meaning that is still there. A handfasting may be just as meaningful to you, or a ceremony you have written yourselves and which you go through after the legal system has been satisfied. No matter what the words or the faith, the inner meaning is the same and it is still a Rite of Passage for you, Daughter of Eve.

When you speak your words of commitment say them slowly and with full understanding of their meaning. No one can know what the future will bring. It may indeed be 'until death do you part', it may part you sooner than you would wish, it may be that you will decide to part within a few years. BUT, at this moment let it be your hope and your desire that death does not intervene between you until after a long and happy life.

There are people who take love lightly, and marriage as well. They go into it with the idea that . . . oh well, if it does not work out we can always get a divorce. This invalidates the ceremony from the start. Such people are not to be trusted with love, and will one day realise their loss.

Motherhood

The next Rite of Passage is that of giving birth. Becoming a Mother is a strange and nerve-wracking process that is totally different for each woman. It is also a passage rite that is beset by a strange creature called the 'Old Wife', and she has tales to tell. The thing is that this Old Wife takes a delight in scaring young mothers and mothers to be with tales of her own confinement(s) (all come equipped with intimate and often gory details). You can well do without this creature even if she lurks under the guise of your mother's oldest and dearest friend. Even one's own mother can have a touch of the Old Wife at times.

Remember one thing: untold millions of women have given birth since the world began and more, millions more, have got through it safely than those that did not. Your body is specially designed to create, build and birth babies. If you prepare well for the event, if you have no inherited diseases that might possibly be passed on, if you do not smoke (or as little as possible), if you keep alcohol to a minimum and above all, if *you take no drugs*, then your chances of having a fairly straightforward confinement and a healthy baby are very high. If you don't care, and if you put your own needs before those of the baby, then you must expect trouble.

In my book *The Tree of Ecstasy* (Aquarian 1991), there is a ritual for The Calling of a Soul. If you are deliberately calling to you a soul who has been with you before, then this is a good ritual to use. Often souls will seek to return into the physical life to be with loved ones they have known in other lives.

I have written in the chapter on The First Flowing about menstruation being the result of the body preparing to host a child. But long before the tiny embryo begins its journey a different kind of preparation should take place. A baby has few needs really, it can get along without a lot of clothes, or toys, many a newborn has slept in a drawer lined with a blanket, and slept well. What they need more than anything is food, warmth and lots of love, the last being the most important. They are resilient little creatures and can survive surprisingly well, but without love they will give up very quickly and return to the other side of life.

They cannot demand a welcome, but the soul hopes for one. They bring with them a rainbow full of promise that, if things go even moderately well, will give them a happy life. Many never get to see that rainbow.

Every child has a right to a healthy body. If you suspect that you may have a condition that could be passed on to a child, you need to think carefully before offering life to a soul. If everyone who carries such a defective gene sacrificed their chance to give birth and instead adopted a child, within a couple of generations there would be no inherited diseases, the carrier lines would have died out. Having said that it is heartbreakingly hard to tell a couple that they should not have a child, or if they do that it has very little chance of avoiding something like Huntington's chorea, haemophilia or any one of many life-threatening ailments that can be passed from one generation to the next.

Sometimes decisions are forced upon parents at a time when they are most vulnerable. No matter how hard we may try there always seem to be times when the little soul slips away. They are getting fewer; more and more premature babies survive against the odds. But the world gets smaller and has less to offer the rapidly increasing population of the world. Soon we will have to choose between placing a limit upon the size of families, or a world where there is no room to breathe, where there is not enough water and not enough food. The choice is a difficult one to make, and it is not helped by the intractable attitude of some religions.

If you feel the time is right to issue an invitation to a soul, then take some time to get yourself fit and well. Ask your doctor to give you a thorough examination and a blood test. Then set aside a whole month in which to think about and meditate upon the child that will come to you. Just before sleep reach out into the spiritual levels and try to feel if there is one who is longing to return to you.

Record your dreams; they may hold a clue. Try not to decide on a son or a daughter, but choose a shortlist of names for both sexes. It is a small thing but important to have a name ready for your child. It is so much better for a child to be greeted with a loving 'hello John, or Paul, or Jessica or Nichola'. A name is magically important, especially when you have just returned to earth. I have known some people who, a month afterwards, have not yet decided and still call their child 'Baby'. We are learning that even newborn babies are amazingly intelligent and can pick up and retain impressions and even incidents in their first month of life.

I have written for you a small ritual that will act as a preparation for conception. It is called Preparing the Room. Also, a series of meditations and 'building' exercises to do while you are pregnant. It is not a good idea to do ritual work when you are carrying a child, as they are very vulnerable to influence at this stage. The Servants of the Light school has, for a long time, made available a tape with these meditations and exercises for expectant mothers. [1] Now they are given here for you, Daughter of Eve. Use them with safety through your time of carrying. You will find that the Builders are part of the angelic group belonging to the level known to Qabalists as Yesod, the Moon centre, which is sacred to Gabriel the Messenger, the Angel of the Annunciation.

The act of love sets up a vortex of force that acts like a directional tunnel down which the soul is guided until it can enter the fertilised ovum and make the first connection with the physical plane. However, it will not stay there, it will come and go during the nine months of growing, checking to see that the body is growing as it should. Sometimes a spontaneous abortion or miscarriage occurs, and this is when the body is not up to the standards the soul needs for its incarnation. Of course, it is possible for it to make mistakes and not to check up often enough. Then a less than perfect physical vehicle may sometimes be born and the soul will have to endure its incarceration until death releases it.

There is no point in the soul taking possession during the time its body is growing in the womb; it can make better use of its time preparing and learning about the life before it. Even after birth the soul is only periodically 'in' until the child begins to take notice of its surroundings. It may continue to move in and out until the moment of sealing. This is usually a shock, trauma, fright, or sudden adrenalin surge which effectively seals the soul to the physical form. After this it may take a long while before conscious vacation of the body, such as astral projection, can be resumed, if ever. It may not be part of its learning processes in this life.

The angelics can be invoked at the time of birth to help you through that enormously energetic and tiring time. While no one could describe giving birth as pleasurable, it is by no means as bad as it used to be when there was no anaesthetic available and no surgical procedures to help in emergencies. Birth is not painless, it is not dignified, and it is exhausting, but it is an experience like no other, and what pain there is, the mind forgets, closing it away from your immediate memory. All is forgotten when you hold your baby for the first time and welcome it back home with its name and loving words.

Once your child is born you enter upon yet another new phase of your life. It will seem as if you have no time to yourself, this small being will claim all of it for itself. One month after the birth is the time to give thanks to the Goddess. In the Christian religion that is a ceremony known as 'churching': a time, says the church, to be reclaimed from the uncleanliness of childbirth and accepted back into normal life, during which they will tack on a giving of thanks for the birth. The whole of the ritual in this book is a thanksgiving for the birth, for your well-being, for the gift of a healthy child. We do not consider childbirth something that is unclean.

I have also included a Naming ceremony and the introduction of the child to the Goddess. You can of course incorporate the two ceremonies together and make one big celebration. If you wish to leave it for another month and make sure you have really recovered from the birth then you may certainly do so: the criteria is that it happens when you wish it to happen.

At this time of your life the overlaps occur. This is when you begin to reach, as an adult, the times you have already experienced as a child, and your mother experienced when you were born. The most significant of these is when your child reaches its first birthday. Times like these, when there are three generations living and learning and loving in the same cycle, are very precious. If the cycle extends to include a fourth generation, then it moves into a new phase. Three is the number of the Goddess, the Empress, the Mother. Four is the number of the Horned God, the Emperor, the Father. Three is Form, Four is Organised Force.

As the family grows you begin to understand how different each birth is, and each child. A woman who bears a daughter is, to some extent, re-creating herself. A woman who bears a son can get confused, he brings out a different kind of love in her. It is no less a love than that which she has for her daughter, but it is different. He is another kind of human . . . a man in potential. She sees in her little girl a chance to do, to wear, to be what she would have liked for herself. This can be dangerous. It is natural, but nevertheless it can go too far. Your daughter is another person, she is *not* you, she is herself. She may not want to go to ballet lessons, preferring to play football with her brother.

A boy makes a mother nervous; she is inclined to watch him as he sleeps and wonder how she managed to produce something so different to herself. She can anticipate things her daughter will do or say or need. This is not so easy with a boy, although some mothers will attempt to force a son into the mould they want him to occupy. Apron strings are only there until he is old enough to walk alone, then they should be cut. All women come to motherhood new and untried, no matter how many brothers and sisters they had. But you have about 20 years in which to work it out.

Notes

1 The tape, *Meditations for Pregnancy*, is obtainable from:
   SOL
   PO Box 215,
   St Helier,
   Jersey,
   CI, UK,
   price £5.00, postage inclusive

8

THE WARRIOR MAID

Not all women want to be wives and mothers, not all women have a maternal instinct or even like children. For some, fulfilment is the cut and thrust of business, the challenge of building up a career in the profession of her choice. Nowadays this might be as a doctor, a dentist, a lawyer, a politician, or bank manager. She might wish to try starting a business using her own talents.

The world today is your very own oyster, Daughter of Eve. Go out and grab the pearl. *But*, old age can be lonely with no one with whom you can share memories of days gone by. Make sure that what you want will not leave you feeling empty when you are older. There are always younger and more able women coming up in the fast lane. I am not saying that marriage is the thing for you, I am saying take care to form relationships that can outlast your working life. These do not have to be sexual: friendship is a precious thing and if, during your life, you can count five people who will stick with you through tears and laughter, then you are blessed indeed.

Learn not to shut yourself away, or work so hard that you forget to relax and enjoy people's company. You may need them some day. If you have no desire to have children of your own, at least keep in touch with friends who have a family. The occasional outing with them will keep you young and au fait with what the younger set is doing and thinking. This may filter through into your work and your outlook and keep you up to date.

Learn to listen to younger colleagues as you get older, ask for their input and even their advice; you will be pleasantly surprised. Or will you? After all, you were like that when you were young. Above all, train someone to fill in your place so that some part of your personal pattern will go on. Take time to laugh, to go out dancing, to take holidays and, when the mood takes you, to take a lover. If he is younger than you it is a bonus, don't feel guilty about it or take to sneaking around corners in case someone from the office sees you. If you have a toy boy, flaunt him! Let the others in the firm or the office know that you may not see the lower side of thirty again, but you still have what it takes, and more.

A Warrior Maid is her own woman, she is content with herself as she is, she needs no one to finance her or to protect her. She can and should take life as it comes and enjoy it to the full. If you are such a one, Daughter of Eve, never let another woman express sympathy for your unwedded state . . . tell her that you are glad she is happy and fulfilled, because you feel the same way, and you do not need a wedding ring to prove it. Don't hurt her feelings, she may indeed be genuinely concerned for you. But you have chosen your way.

You may have chosen a different way of sexuality. It is your right to do so, you do not have to feel any less a woman. By the same token, allow others the same right without feeling superior. You may not need a man for a lover, you may not think much of them as a sex, but there are some nice guys out there. They make good friends, and once they know you can be a good friend too, there is an opportunity to get together without hassles.

I have given you a ritual for your own, one to give you balance between the Warrior and the Maid. Be strong without being overbearing, as you can be feminine without being weak.

Being free to do as you wish opens up many possibilities for you. Travel and being able to live and work in exotic surroundings is one option. Climbing the ladder to a top executive position is another. You can opt for prising open some of the few doors still closed to women, or at least open them a little wider. We have had a woman Prime Minister, we have a woman Speaker in the House of Commons. We have women ambassadors, women judges and High Court judges. We have women company directors, women producers and heads of film studios, and it probably will not be too long before we see a woman as the President of the USA. Yes, the Warrior Maids can fly far, fast and high.

Cutting the Ties

Sometimes, no matter how hard we try, people who married with such high hopes for the future fall out of love. Often it is because one outgrows the other in some way. Sometimes it is infidelity, lack of trust, money, jealousy, or just plain boredom with each other. It can be anyone of these or a dozen other and different reasons.

Separation and divorce are getting to be almost normal. Marriages stand less and less chance of succeeding. Some struggle to remain together for the sake of their children, it is a moot point if this is better or worse for them. But people feel they have to try.

Sometimes the marriage is doomed from the beginning because two people are seen around a lot together and people begin to think of them as a couple. Soon they begin to feel pressurised, they take on other people's ideas of what they are to each other. Finally, they feel that they might as well get married, after all they know each other and they are good together, and so on and so forth. It never works. If the spark is not there the fire will not burn.

In many countries, marriages are still arranged. In India an astrologer is often called in to set up charts for two people; if the charts do not agree they cannot be married. The Stars say no. Even in parts of Europe marriages are still arranged because land and money and bloodlines are involved. It used to happen a great deal in Spain, though not so much now. I remember a Spaniard telling me that his bride had been promised to him when she was only twelve and he nineteen. They were distantly related and the vast tracts of land in Andalucia would be kept in the family. 'Love will come after the marriage', he told me. 'It will come because it will have to do so. We must live together for the rest of our lives. There has never been a divorce in our family. We will work hard to find good things about each other that we can like. The children will be the cement in our marriage.'

In other parts of Europe, in England and in America, such conditions would almost certainly doom the marriage to failure. There are times when it seems a marriage must fail, but with hard work and determination it can be saved. One should always try, but equally there are times when it must be allowed to founder, because there is nothing left on which to build. This is always a tragedy when there are children, especially if they are young. They simply do not understand why they do not see one of their parents any more, or at least as frequently as they did before.

All too often in places where marriages are taken too lightly and become too frequent, the children hardly have time to get to know a step-parent before he or she disappears and another takes their place. To be honest it is not always their fault. We who live and work within the framework of the occult are very aware of the power of thought. Take Hollywood, for example. People like film and theatre stars who live their lives in the full glare of the public are susceptible to thoughts and thought forms. Young people, especially adolescents with their enormous energy levels, fix their minds and thoughts on such people and daydream about them, sometimes using them as sexual dream partners. This fuels a particularly jealous thought form. When sent out on to the astral, such thought forms seek out and attach themselves to their real counterparts. The weight of such dream forms can sap the energy and ability of that person to form any kind of real and lasting relationship.

It is this kind of thing that ruins the lives of pop stars and singers. Some avoid it by not marrying at all. As soon as they do, the millions of thought forms generated by jealous fans take action and the wife or husband is pushed to one side and eventually the marriage is destroyed.

What happens when love dies and only the shell of the marriage is left? How do you know when it has gone? It may seem a trivial thing, but one of the most reliable pointers to a dead marriage is when you stop eating together. Sharing food in everyday life is as much a sacrament as taking communion. Food, bread and salt sustain life, being won from the earth by hard work. We offer food at Harvest Time, we offer food to those who come visiting. In Middle-Eastern countries someone visiting for the first time is offered bread and salt and water. Food shared has a mystical meaning, and when a relationship breaks down this is one of the first things to go. When food is no longer shared, the closeness has gone.

Preparing, cooking and presenting food has always been thought of as one of the main aspects of housewifery, as the priestess of the Hearth Fire, the Nephthys of the Cup of Hospitality. Yet some of the most famous cooks of the world are men. A lot of men enjoy cooking as both a hobby and as a means of relaxing. My husband Michael is a first-class cook who thoroughly enjoys chopping and slicing and grating. He regards it along the lines of Alchemy, and will spend hours blending tastes, colours and spices. I can produce an edible meal but have little interest in domestic chores such as cooking. Cordon Bleu is lost on me as I like my food well cooked but plain, and rarely notice much of what is before me. I prefer to write and talk. But Michael and I complement each other in what we enjoy doing, and we share the cooking as far as is possible.

Loss of interest in the home that a couple has built together is another symptom of the breakdown of a marriage. If there are no children then it may be better to part and to give each other time to find other partners with whom they may be better suited to build a family life. No matter what has been the cause of the break-up, try hard not to let it end with bitterness and recrimination. This is not always possible when feelings have been deeply hurt and vows taken lightly or broken completely.

Sometimes we learn a great deal from a first marriage, things that help us to make a second marriage more successful, stable and mutually growth orientated. Once a union has broken down completely it is better to let it go and learn from the experience, painful though it may be. The arc threads that were there at the beginning wither and die of their own accord, but there is still a need to ritually write 'finish' and free each other from lingering doubts, anger and feelings of guilt.

Those who have been trained, even if only partially, in the way of the mysteries will know that to harbour such feelings can only keep parts of an unsatisfactory union alive, though barely. If this is allowed to happen, inevitably it binds the two people concerned in chains of their own making. It then becomes the Tarot card of The Devil: illusion, self-deceit, and inertia.

If there is still something to fight for, then fight on; if there is nothing left, then go and don't look back. The ritual I have given for cutting these marital ties is short and sharp, as it must be. It is time to choose a new road on which to travel, one with a new goal and new experiences. Another Tarot card springs to mind here, it is The Star.

9

THE RITUALS

The Wedding Day

This is just a short personal ritual that a bride might like to do early on the morning of her wedding day, before everyone arrives and starts taking charge!

At dawn, rise and greet the day by opening the window. Even if it is cold take a few minutes to greet the first light of the day, a day that is very special to you. If it is warm leave the window open, or better still if you have a garden go down and sit for a few minutes in the silence and the peace that is always found as the new day breaks.

Think about your life as a child, recall the happy days, and choose one day in particular to go over in as much detail as you can remember. Compare the child you were to the young bride you are now. Call to the younger self that you once were and thank her. Thank your inner child and bless her, tell her that when you have children of your own you will remember her with love and gratitude for what you learned in those far off days. The inner child is an important part of every human being – to forget it is to allow something precious to die.

Take some loose hair from your head and whisper a wish into it, then hold it up and let the wind take it away. Share your happiness with the whole house, the garden, the people who are beginning to wake up. Let your love and your blessing flow over and through the whole house.

To seal this day you might like to do one of two things. You might like to buy a gift – something beautiful, a special doll, a pretty dress, a pair of shoes, anything pretty – something a little girl would love. Take it to an orphanage near to you,

or maybe a Dr Barnado's Home or a hospital, and ask for it
to be given to a little girl as a thanksgiving for your own
childhood. Alternatively, you might like to help support a
child in a Third World country by giving a small amount of
money each month. Then some child, somewhere, will have
a chance they might not have had, to live a little better. It is
only a little thing, but it is a thanks offering for what *you had
as a child*.

This does not of course have to be done right away, unless
you wish to arrange it to coincide with your wedding. Lastly,
you might like to think about having your wedding bouquet
made with a small detachable posy, or spray of flowers. As
well as the invited guests all sorts of people turn up to watch
a wedding, and you will always find one or two old ladies
watching with wistful faces, perhaps remembering their own
wedding day, or the one they never had because it may have
been just after World War Two and there was no money, or
indeed clothing coupons to spare. Spare the posy for someone
like that, share your joy with an older woman and make her
remember the past. In giving, you will receive a thousandfold.

Preparing the Room
When the time comes and the two of you decide to begin your
family I hope you will have already taken my advice to get
your body as healthy as you can. Remember that *you* are the
source of all the building materials that will go into making
your baby. What you eat, what you have stored in your body,
the quality of your personal health, will determine the
strength and well-being of the newcomer.

Begin to record your dreams if you do not already do so. It
may be that the souls that wait on the other side of life for
invitations to be born will try to touch your heart and mind.
The Lords of Light that guide our destinies may have decided
to send someone special into your life, or they may simply
stand aside and let a soul come to you.

Each night before you sleep the two prospective parents
should send out a call to the soul that will eventually become
their child. Keep calling and it will use your vibrations like a
map to guide it to the time and the place when it will begin
its move into the physical level.

It is best not to try and impose a definite sex upon the soul.

It may need to be a male when you want a female, or vice versa. Instead, simply offer it love and a welcome into your home and your life.

Place a small table between you, covered with a white cloth on which stands either a white candle in a holder, or a nightlight in a deep blue bowl. Also a small glass of wine, and one grain of rice on a white napkin. The bowl represents the Great Mother, the Virgin Mother of the Son of the Sun. The Light symbolises the Sun Child. Sit either side of the table and hold hands. Look into the flame and visualise the face of The Mother. She stands in a garden filled with white flowers holding in Her arms the soul of the child destined to come to you.

Woman: GREAT MOTHER OF THE LOVING HEART, WE OPEN OUR LIVES AND OUR BODIES TO THE SOUL YOU HOLD IN YOUR ARMS. IF THAT SOUL IS ONE WHO HAS BEEN A PART OF OUR LIVES BEFORE, THEN WE WILL WELCOME IT BACK, IF IT IS NEWLY SENT TO US, THEN IT IS STILL WELCOME. WE HAVE PREPARED OURSELVES FOR THIS MOMENT WITH MEDITATION AND PRAYER, WE LOOK TO THE FUTURE WITH HOPE AND JOY. I OFFER MY WOMB TO THE SOUL AND THEREIN I SHALL WEAVE A BODY FOR ITS PHYSICAL CLOTHING.

IN THE TIME OF MY DELIVERY I WILL CALL UPON YOU FOR HELP AND SUPPORT. BE WITH ME THEN AS THE SOUL ENTERS INTO LIFE.

Man: MOTHER OF THE SUN CHILD, I OFFER MY LIFE FORCE TO HELP CREATE THE BODY FOR THIS SOUL THAT WAITS FOR US TO SUMMON IT INTO THE WORLD. I WILL BE ITS PROTECTOR AND ITS GUARDIAN WHILE IT IS YOUNG. I WILL TRY TO TEACH THE CHILD THOSE THINGS IT SHOULD KNOW TO BE WORTHY OF THE LIFE IT HAS BEEN GIVEN. WHEN THE TIME COMES I WILL SET THE CHILD'S FEET UPON ITS OWN PATH THAT IT MAY WALK THE PATH OF ITS DESTINY. BE WITH ME AS I TRY TO UNDERSTAND THE CHILD'S NEEDS. I WILL SHARE ITS JOYS AND SORROWS AND TRY TO TEACH PATIENCE AND TOLERANCE, AND ABOVE ALL, A LOVE OF LIFE. (The man now places the grain of rice into the wine and blesses it.)

THIS CUP OF WINE I TAKE TO BE THE SYMBOL OF THE
WELCOMING WOMB OF WOMAN, THE GRAIN OF RICE
THE SEED THAT WILL CAUSE IT TO BECOME FERTILE
WITH THE PHYSICAL BODY OF THE CHILD WE SO
DESIRE. BLESSED BE THIS CUP AND THE WINE WITHIN,
BLESSED BE THE GRAIN OF RICE THAT IT MAY
SYMBOLISE MY SEED. BLESSED BE THIS MOMENT IN
TIME.
(Gives cup to woman to drink.)

Do this three nights in a row, just before the most fertile time
of the woman's moon cycle. During daytime the woman
should follow a pathworking that will prepare the place for
her child. Settle yourself comfortably and relax, breathe
slowly and deeply and go over each part of your body,
tightening and relaxing until you are feeling 'boneless'. Now
begin your working. Imagine that you are drawing back inside
your head, deeper and deeper until you come to a halt. At first
it is dark, but then you see a small light flickering in the
darkness. You move towards it and it gets bigger. Finally, you
see that it is a lantern hanging on a nail at the top of a spiral
stairway.

Take hold of the lantern and begin to descend. Round and
round you go, holding the lantern up to guide your steps. On
the walls are pictures, paintings, and as you look at them you
begin to realise that they are pictures of your life going
backwards in time as you descend into your inner self. From
time to time you may wish to stop and look at a particular
picture and remember things.

At last, the stairway comes to an end and before you is a
corridor, slightly curved and panelled in red velvet. It leads
to a point where it is joined by another corridor of similar
nature. They both empty into a shorter corridor, also
decorated in deep red, and at the end of this is a door.

When you open the door it leads into an empty room. It is
not very big but is light and airy with two small, mullioned
windows looking out on to a garden. In the room is a step
ladder, tins of paint and brushes, a strong wooden table and
a colour chart. You will also find, hanging behind the door,
a pair of overalls. Look through the colour chart and decide
what colour you would like to paint the ceiling and the

woodwork of this room. Take your time and when you have decided you will find that the tins of paint are exactly that colour. Leave the room now and return to your own level of consciousness.

Once or twice a week you may go down to the room and paint it until it is all done. Try and make the painting as real an experience as you can. It should take you about a month. You might miss a few days. Once the painting is done you will find on your next visit rolls of paper and a trestle table, brushes and paste waiting for you. Or, if you would rather have painted walls, you will find more tins of the colour you prefer. Again do it slowly and not more than twice a week. One thing you will find is that although your physical body is getting bigger, your inner body remains the same. When you have finished you will find the room carpeted when you next come.

Now you can begin to move in the furniture: a rocking chair; a larger armchair with a footstool; a sheepskin rug; a wardrobe with shelves; a small chest of drawers; a changing table and a crib. You will also find shelving that you can fill with toys, a mobile hanging over the crib, and in one corner a small wash basin. Each time you visit, the room will have added something. You can change what you do not want or like and add anything you feel you will need.

Now the room is ready for the curtains, you will find a sewing machine, cottons, needles and material to choose from: everything you need to make curtains and covers for cushions, and perhaps hangings for the crib. Once the room is finished you can go there and sit and think about your baby. It does not matter that in the everyday world you have to make do with a room less than this, here in your inner world the room represents your womb and here the babe can grow in love and safety. When you go into labour it may help if you descend to this room where you will find your baby lying in the crib. Pick it up and bring it back with you. The Builders will come with you, helping you to get back to the foot of the stairs and climb up them to the 'finish line'.

Meditations For Pregnancy

No ritual work should be undertaken by a pregnant woman, other than meditation and gentle pathworkings. Full-scale ritual has an effect upon the endocrine system and this in turn can upset the delicate balance of the creation that is going on inside you. Also there is the fact that we now know that babies in the womb can 'feel' emotionally and be affected by emotion. Ritual is fuelled by emotions and therefore it might be harmful to the child. The symbiotic relationship between mother and child is so strong that what affects her will inevitably affect the baby. There are other reasons but they need to be gone into as part of an on-going training session and need more time than we have here.

It is a special time for both the people concerned – they are, quite literally wrapped up in each other, communing in a special way and all the woman's time, thoughts, and feelings are centred on her condition. In occult teachings we have the axiom of 'as above, so below'. Here we have it expressed in a different way: 'The Child within and the Mother without'. It is a mystical union every bit as powerful as that mystical union that brought the child into being in the first place.

The work best done while pregnant is that which is tuned towards those beings known as The Builders. They are concerned with Form and the building of all forms. They are in fact the angelic servants of those mighty beings we call The Lords of Form, the Elohim. As such they are also a part of the archetype of The Great Mother, or Binah the primal giver of all Form.

Meditations aimed towards contact with these beings are beneficial to the growing embryo. It encourages the tiny ego to become aware of the love and powerful creating energies of these beings. We tend to think of such beings as always around helping and encouraging humanity. But this is not so, there is the Law of Free Will involved. In order to have free will we must give up being cosseted. So even these gentle and powerful energies must be asked for their help before they can give it. To simply help without being asked would be an infringement of our free will.

It is a source of pain to them that at times they can only stand by and look on, like children outside a house where a party is going on, wanting to be there, to join in, but having to wait until asked.

In the following pages you will find exercises, meditations and guided workings all tuned to your special needs at this time. We in the Servants of the Light School have been using them for pregnant students for nearly twenty years and they have never had any unwanted effects. As soon as a woman student becomes pregnant, she stops the course lessons and goes on to these. Only when the birth is over, the child is sleeping through the night and the mother has fully recovered, does she return to the course lessons.

There is no rigid timetable for these workings. They are for you to do when you have time, when you are feeling relaxed, or on the verge of sleep. That is best of all, since as you drift into sleep the exercises and meditations will continue on the higher levels.

Short ten-minute sessions are better than a long thirty-minute one. As your girth increases it gets harder to sit for very long in one position, harder still to be fully comfortable in any position. So two or three short sessions are better for you. Neither is there any need to keep records unless you wish to do so. With regard to position, you may find lying down on a couch or settee with a rolled-up towel under the small of your back and another under your knees will give you more support. Also a neckrest of the kind used when flying is very useful. This means that the body is supported in a series of gentle curves at each of the main pressure points.

Although pathworkings may be considered to be a minor form of ritual it does not need the amount of emotional input that a ritual needs. Therefore it does not place undue pressure on the child. Always begin with some relaxation exercises, either those given at the pre-natal classes, or those in the SOL course. [1]

Meditation One

We begin with the following exercise: put a small fresh loaf on a plate in front of you where you can see it without strain. Look at it and think of all the processes that went into its making, and before, right back to its sowing as seed in the ground. Work backwards. See in your mind the bread being taken from the oven, warm and soft. Capture the smell of fresh baking.

Go back to the moment when it was placed in the oven.

Now think of the mixing process, the flour, the yeast, the salt, everything that goes into the making of it. In one sense it is an alchemical process, just as the process that produces the child you carry was, in its purest form, an alchemical process. Genetic material from you and from your partner was combined to begin a mixture of DNA that will result, in a few months, in a new and original human being. Carry this process of imagination right back, in stages, to the moment when the farmer sowed his field with corn seed. As the yeast rises and grows, it forms a parallel with your own body as it grows and swells. This is building in a very real sense.

Meditation Two

Think of a chalice, take your time and build it carefully. A plain, simple chalice. It holds a bunch of grapes, filling it to overflowing and hanging down the side. Grapes and the vine from which they come are an ancient symbol. The Vine signifies the Divine King who rules for a while and then gives up his life for his people, his blood becoming the red wine. Since the king is always regarded as being of a dual nature, divine and human, he is also the bread, the corn king cut down and offered as a sacred food.

In a sense your child has made a sacrifice in order to take on a physical form. It has given up a high state of life and descended into a lower one. The wine of love is the link between you and your partner and your child. Think of yourself as the vine. Heavy with fruit and sweetness. Think of the other vines that surround you, all with fruit, they are a symbol of all the children that have ever been and will be.

Here you have a link right through history. Now, in your imagination fill the chalice with water. As you do so think of the great tides of the oceans as they rise and fall, governed by the Moon, as you, a woman, are governed by the Moon each month. At the moment those tides are stilled within you but they will come again. Think also of the tides of the seasons as they move through the years, spring and sowing, summer and growing, autumn and harvest, winter and sleep.

Think of the great waves of the sea and remember them

when you go into labour and use this image and the strength of those waves to help you as the contractions ebb and flow. See the Moon reflected in this chalice, like a moonboat sailing the night sky, bringing your child ever nearer to your arms. Now fill the chalice with the smoke of incense and watch it rise up and wreathe around the stem. Think of the first breath your child will take at the moment of birth, taken from its watery element into the light and the air of its first day of life.

Fill the chalice with the flame of the phoenix and see the promise of life beyond life and all that this means in terms of linkage with you and with others past, present and future. Your child is a living part of a line that stretches from this moment right back to an aeon-distant creature floating in a warm sea under a very new sun.

Now fill your chalice with wine, think of yourself as the chalice and the child as the wine of love, for you are both a part of the Great Vine, the Son of the Sun. Now absorb the chalice and the wine into yourself and let them fill you both with its power and its strength.

Meditation Three
Think of an oyster shell deep in the ocean, lying quietly in a safe corner between the rocks. Deep within, a process is taking place that is similar to the one that is happening within you. A pearl is being formed. A small intrusion, similar to a single sperm, has penetrated the soft inner secrets of the oyster, generating the creation of a beautiful pearl around this 'seed'. Meditate on this image and watch the pearl grow. Finally have the shell open wide, reach in and take the pearl, and absorb it into your body where it seeks out the child and gently inserts itself into the third eye. The pearl of wisdom will remain there.

Meditation Four
Choose a favourite piece of music: classical or semi-classical, or perhaps traditional music. Listen to it and allow it to form pictures in your mind.

If you cannot stand classical music at all, then choose quiet melodic music that will soothe the child, for be sure that it will hear it. Hearing is the first sense to come into full use. As an extension of this meditation, search out a picture that appeals to you and use it as a starting point for a pathworking. Move into the picture and explore its environment. This works especially well with cottage garden pictures or landscapes.

Meditation and Pathworking

Build in the mind a small temple of very simple design. It has four stained-glass windows, one in each quarter, and a black and white squared floor. A white marble altar stands in the middle with a Chalice of wine on it. Behind the altar stand four slightly larger-than-life beings. Their colours are Rose, Amber Gold, Green and deep Blue. They are of the Order of the Builders, the servants of the Elohim. They are here to help and protect you and your child until after the birth. It is their task to see that all goes well.

Move to the altar and stand before it and summon the figure in Rose to stand before you. It comes and bows. Ask it for a name and when you receive the name ask the being to help you through your pregnancy. It will agree and you will share wine from the cup. Now call the figure in Amber Gold and repeat the sequence. Then the one in Green and finally the one in Blue. These beings are now assigned to you and will be with you right through your time until the birth.

Pathworking: The World Mother

Let us go together upon a journey that will be as near as your own heartbeat and as far as the most distant star. We are going to see a great Being to ask for knowledge of the future and for the child within you. See before us the Doorway that becomes a part of the wall before you. It opens and we can see a green meadow filled with flowers. Rise and walk through into the Summerworld with me.

The grass is cool and slightly damp beneath our feet, and there are daisies and meadowsweet, buttercups and coltsfoot covering the whole field. There is a little path that winds across the fields and leads towards some trees wearing their full summer dress of leaves and flowers. A small rabbit stops to stare as we go past and the birds chatter from the branches, asking where we are going. There is a special glow about those who take the road to the mountain of vision, and it is shining from our faces now.

In the distance we can see some other people, an older couple and a young man, and they join us, talking eagerly of seeing the sacred mountain. We cross a stream and sit for a while in the shade of an old, forgotten orchard. The apples there are small but sweet and very refreshing, and after a rest we are soon on our way again. A young woman with a small child carried on her hip joins us. She has another child running beside her. You feel well and strong and to pass the time we start to sing old country songs and nursery rhymes as we walk along. A farmer leaning on his gate asks if he may join the party. We say yes, and he whistles to his dog and comes along. Soon he takes the child from her mother and gives her a ride on his broad shoulders.

A woman washing clothes in the stream leaves her washing and runs after us calling, 'Do not leave me, I will come with you, please, please wait'.

We leave the green fields and come to a small dusty road leading towards a blue misty ridge of mountains in the distance. At the next turn in the road we meet a boy riding a big Shire horse, who takes the older child in front of him, turns the horse to follow us, and off we go again. We pass through villages where the people offer us fresh-baked bread and home-made cheese and draughts of sweet ale and cider. Others drive us out with harsh words, and throw stones at us. The older woman starts to falter and the young boy gets down from the horse and, with the farmer's help, gets her up on its broad back. Then he walks alongside, holding the horse's head and leading it gently. Soon you are getting tired with the weight of the child within you, so you too are helped onto the broad back of the big Shire and we travel on.

The evening comes slowly and the light dims. A wind springs up and the younger child begins to weep. Soon the light has gone and we walk, silently now, in the early evening darkness. The older couple are weary, the old lady is walking again now, but they insist on keeping up with us. The farmer calls to his dog and says he will go back – it is too far, he will miss his evening meal and his wife will worry. The man and his dog disappear into the twilight and the sound of their going dies away. The next to leave is the young man. He explains that he cannot leave his mother alone at night and feels he must return to her, perhaps another time he will go with us the whole way, but not tonight. Keep your heart high, the journey will be worth it. I will not let you fall or stumble.

We walk silently now. The horse is weary and plods with its head held low. The old woman is nodding, almost asleep on her feet. The mother is carrying her youngest child asleep on her breast, while I carry the older child. We are all tired and hungry. Then the mountains loom up suddenly before us, we had not realised that we had got so close to them.

The laundress leaves us now. She says she must get back and have the washing done for her family. They will wonder where she has gone and will be looking for her. Also, there is no one to cook dinner for them so she must go. She will look for us when we return and perhaps we can tell her what the rest of the journey was like. She turns and runs off into the night and the sound of her running feet dies away. The young mother sits down beside the road and seems too weak to go much further. Rest against my shoulder.

Borne on the night breeze we can hear a faint song, sweet and loving. It reminds each one of us of a time when we lay at rest within our mothers' arms, safe and secure. We cannot make out the words but the far-off voice seems to promise warmth and care and shelter. Weary but determined, we move on. Even the horse seems to have regained some strength.

Now we set foot on the mountain path and start to climb. The winds are strong and cold, and there is little shelter, but we move on, working our way steadily upwards. Don't be afraid, I will help you. At last, the horse can go no further and the boy slips its halter from its drooping head, turns it round and, with a pat, sends it down towards the road far below and the sweet grass beside it. We turn our faces to the mountain and begin to climb. Once more I will hold your hand, the boy now carries the older child.

We feel we are almost at the end of our strength when we see a cave opening before us. Gratefully we enter it, thinking to find shelter for the night, but it is bare and damp. However, it seems to go deeper and we follow it into the heart of the mountain. Now we can hear the voice again, nearer and clearer than before. We stumble along, feeling our way in the darkness. Will we never come to the end of our journey?

Ahead we can see a light, and the voice, speaking now, bids us come close. Cautiously, we move forward and come out into a great underground temple. A fire burns in a firepit, giving off a strange but pleasant perfume. Willing but unseen hands help us move to the warmth. We are given a hot drink and some food and the invisible presences tell us to rest awhile. The children and the old people revive in the pleasant warmth and even find the energy to talk a little. We wait patiently and soon the same soft but unseen hands guide us into a short, dark passage and from there into a place of softness, as if it were lined with feathers. We cannot see in the warm darkness, but we feel safe and cared for. The same soft murmuring voice we heard before bids us closer and we move forward to be enveloped into welcoming arms and held against a warm, soft breast. Cradled against this great nurturing Being we feel at rest and at peace, we are in the presence of The World Mother. The voice starts to sing again and in that song we hear our lives laid out before us: We are told of our strengths and our weaknesses, of what lies before us and how we must cope with what life will bring. The old people are shown their youth and offered a chance to return to it. The young woman is shown her children grown. Tall and strong, their lives will be given to the care of others. The boy is shown the way whereby he may climb to great wealth and two ways to use it – for the good of others or for himself; he will have to choose which way he will go. And what of us? What does the dream hold for us? For you it shows the sweet face of the babe within you and the face of the father. A ring of stars dances around your child's head and one of them falls down into its eyes and disappears into its thoughts. That star will surface as a gift from the World Mother when it is older.

Now we are shown the face of She who holds us, a vast, sad face, as old as time and young as a May morning. She is winged and her breast is soft with downy feathers. She is both beautiful and ugly, harsh and loving. She is the Primal Mother and all who come to Her may rest one night upon Her breast and learn of their future. We learn of what lies before us, of the trials ahead and the victories. We learn of times to beware and times to rejoice. We learn of the seasons in our lives and the reaping and sowing that is all of our own doing. Those who are soon to be mothers rest easy in Her arms and are shown their babes as they will be when they are born. They receive strength and wisdom and understanding for they are the true daughters of the World Mother. They will always be dear to her heart.

Slowly and gently we sleep, rest and dream. In the early morning we are awoken by the unseen hands. They guide us out of the cave temple and into the fresh chilly morning of a new day. We stand and look down below and see far away the Shire horse cropping the grass by the roadside and the smoke from the villages just beyond the foothills.

We start down the path and then stop. The old people are not with us. We retrace our steps but the cave has gone and there is nothing to show that it was ever there. We look at each other and nod wisely, we know that they have chosen to return to youth, to rebirth, and that even now they lie sleeping on the breast of the World Mother, waiting for their time to come again. They smile in their sleep and dream of the life to come.

Walking briskly to keep away the cold, we make our way down from the mountain, and are soon making our way back to where we started. The horse, refreshed by a night's rest, clip clops along with the children on his back. They laugh and chatter and have no cares, the dreams they were shown are but dreams to them, as yet. But the young mother is silent and thinks deeply on what has been revealed to her. The young boy is also silent and we wonder what he will choose to do with the knowledge he has been given.

What of you, you who have taken this path to the World Mother? What was the Star Gift to your child? You must wait and see. But always the World Mother will watch over you. We walk on and as we walk, the scene fades and we find ourselves walking back through the Doorway which led us into this world.

The Blessing Ceremony

The last of these exercises is the blessing ceremony (this is not on the SOL tape mentioned earlier). Return to the temple, where you will see a ring of figures, all of whom are of the same order of Beings as the four now assigned to you. They are dressed in every colour of the rainbow. In the centre of the temple is a solid, comfortable chair with a footstool. One of the figures escorts you to the chair and you sit.

From somewhere in the distance a choir of sweet voices begins to chant. Light plays through the stained glass of the windows and a feeling of deep peace comes over you. One by one each figure (there are seven) comes forward and kneels before you. You may ask it for a gift for the child you carry. It may agree, or it may say that in this life that particular gift is not possible, but it will offer another in its place. When all have approached you, you will be escorted out of the temple into a garden filled with flowers. There are pathways and little hidden arbours, pools full of fish and avenues of trees. You may come here whenever you wish, and there will always be something new for you to discover.

Giving Thanks, and the Naming

Once your child is born, life will never be the same – time becomes a commodity that is always in short supply. The amount of attention, time, washing and care one small baby needs is amazing. You will get tired very easily and you may be one of those mothers who gets a bout of depression a few weeks after the birth. Make sure that you get advice about this and don't think you can cope on your own.

Once the baby is sleeping through the night and you feel more like your old self you might like to think about Giving Thanks, and maybe combining it with a Naming Ritual. Today not everyone wants a church christening, it is not compulsory and those with a New Age or pagan frame of mind prefer to do things their own way.

If the weather is warm enough then both rites can be held out of doors, but a very young baby will need to be kept warm. In that case your own living room or any area large enough to hold those people you wish to invite will be the best choice. If it is high summer then you can use the same rituals but simply extend the festivities to include dancing as well as the music, etc.

The Thanksgiving
You need to give thanks to round off the whole process of birth. The angelics, the Builders, the Great Mother, the Fairy Folk, in fact whomsoever you asked for help during your time of creation. All of them need to be given some kind of

recognition for their help. Make an altar from a table, lay it with a cloth and fill it with flowers. You will also need a large white candle which you should anoint with anointing oil, then wind a white satin ribbon around it in a spiral and tie off.

Put a central light in the middle, add a small loaf of home-baked bread, a chalice of wine or non-alcoholic grape juice, some bird seed and nuts, a large bowl of mixed wild flower seeds and bulbs, a young tree ready for planting, and a rose bush. You will also need a little salt, some pure rain water or water from a sacred well (if you live near London the Jordanian embassy often has small bottles of Jordan water available for christenings), otherwise water from the Chalice well or the Walsingham spring. A small amount of pure oil will be needed as well.

An older woman acts as the priestess and brings the young mother to the altar and instructs her to kneel.

Priestess: CHILD OF THE MOTHER WHY DO YOU COME TO THIS ALTAR?

Mother: TO GIVE THANKS FOR MY TIME OF CARRYING AND FOR THE SAFE DELIVERY OF MY CHILD.

Priestess: TO WHOM DO YOU GIVE THESE THANKS?

Mother: TO THE GODDESS, TO THE MOTHER, TO HER HELPERS WHO WERE WITH ME ALL THROUGH MY TIME OF CREATING.

Priestess: WHAT DO YOU OFFER HER AND THEM?

Mother: I OFFER THINGS TO MAKE HER WORLD MORE BEAUTIFUL. I OFFER SEEDS AND BULBS FOR THE EARTH, FOOD FOR THE BIRDS AND BEASTS, AND FOR THE MOTHER A ROSE, THE MOST BEAUTIFUL OF ALL FLOWERS AND DEAREST TO HER HEART, TO BE PLANTED IN THE GOOD EARTH AND TENDED BY ME AS A SACRED DUTY. I BRING MY CHILD TO BE WASHED AND ANOINTED AND GIVEN SALT AND WINE AND TO BE NAMED IN THE ANCIENT WAY.

Priestess: IN THE NAME OF THE GREAT MOTHER I ACCEPT THESE THINGS AND BLESS THEM WITH PURE WATER. (sprinkles them) I BLESS THE SALT, CASTING OUT FROM IT ALL THAT IS IMPURE AND CALLING IN ALL THAT IS GOOD. (turns to mother) I SPRINKLE YOU WITH WATER THAT YOU MAY GROW IN GRACE AND BEAUTY

AND UNDERSTANDING. (sprinkles a few drops on her head) I GIVE YOU BREAD AND SALT TO BIND YOU TO THE MOTHER FOR THE BREAD IS GROWN IN HER FRUITFUL BODY, AND THE SALT IS GATHERED FROM HER OCEAN. LASTLY I GIVE YOU WINE AS A TOKEN OF HER COMMUNION WITH YOU, HER DAUGHTER. (gives wine)

LET THE FATHER COME FORTH. (father comes to kneel before her) SON OF THE MOTHER, WHY DO YOU COME TO THIS ALTAR?

Father: TO GIVE THANKS FOR THE SAFE DELIVERY OF OUR CHILD, AND THE COURAGE OF MY WIFE IN HER PAIN.

Priestess: TO WHOM DO YOU GIVE THESE THANKS?

Father: TO THE GODDESS, THE MOTHER, AND TO THOSE WHO HELPED DURING THE NINE MONTHS OF CREATING.

Priestess: WHAT TO YOU OFFER?

Father: I OFFER A YOUNG TREE, TO BE PLANTED IN THE EARTH, TO BE A LIVING COMPANION TO THE CHILD, TO GROW WITH IT YEAR BY YEAR IN STRENGTH AND GRACE.

Priestess: IN THE NAME OF THE MOTHER I BLESS THIS TREE, THAT IT MAY GROW LIKE THE CHILD TALL AND STRONG AND HEALTHY. I BLESS THE FATHER IN HIS STRENGTH AND CARING. (sprinkles with water and give bread and salt) I GIVE YOU WINE AS A TOKEN OF THE COMMUNION BETWEEN YOU AND THE MOTHER.

Gives wine. Both rise and the child is brought to the altar, if warm enough it should be naked, or wrapped in pure silk.

The Naming

Priestess: WHO BRINGS THIS CHILD TO THE ALTAR OF THE MOTHER?

Parents: WE BRING THE CHILD TO THE ALTAR.

Priestess: FOR WHAT PURPOSE?

Parents: TO BE NAMED ACCORDING TO THE ANCIENTS WAYS.

Priestess: WHAT ARE THOSE WAYS?

Parents: ONE NAME FOR THE EVERYDAY WORLD, ONE NAME FOR THE TREE COMPANION, AND ONE NAME TO

BE KEPT UNTIL THE CHILD IS READY.

Priestess: WHAT IS THE EVERYDAY NAME?

Parents: (speak child's everyday name)

Priestess: WHAT IS THE NAME OF THE COMPANION?

Parents: (speak companion's name)

Priestess: PASS ME THE SECRET NAME (they hand her a slip of paper) SECRET UNTIL THE RIGHT TIME SHALL COME, ONLY THE MOTHER WILL KNOW. (burns slip of paper in flame and puts pinch of ashes into the wine. Lights the birthday candle.) CHILD OF THE GREAT MOTHER, THIS CANDLE IS YOUR BIRTH CANDLE, YOUR NAMING CANDLE AND ON THIS DAY EACH YEAR IT WILL BE LIT FOR A FEW MINUTES. WITH ITS FLAME I WIND THE PROTECTION OF THE MOTHER ABOUT YOU.

The child is held out by the father and the priestess passes the candle over and round the child in a spiral motion from head to foot.

I PLACE UPON YOUR TONGUE SACRED AND BLESSED SALT, THAT YOU KNOW THE SALT OF HER OCEANS FROM WHENCE ALL LIFE HAS COME. (sprinkles a few grains of salt on baby's tongue) I SPRINKLE YOU WITH CLEAR WATER AND NAME YOU .... FOR YOURSELF, AND .... FOR YOUR COMPANION. YOUR THIRD NAME WILL BE TOLD TO YOU WHEN THE TIME IS RIGHT. I GIVE YOU WINE AS YOUR FIRST COMMUNION WITH THE GODDESS (dips finger in wine and place on baby's lips) WITH OIL I ANOINT YOU (top of head, breast and feet) AND I PRESENT YOU TO THE MOTHER. (takes and holds child up to the East, then the South, then West, and finally North)

GREAT MOTHER TAKE THIS CHILD .... UNDER YOUR PROTECTION AND GRANT HER/HIM LONG LIFE, HEALTH AND HAPPINESS. LET PROSPERITY PAVE THE WAY BEFORE HER/HIM, BUT MAY HER/HIS HEART ALWAYS BE MINDFUL OF THE NEEDS OF OTHERS. THE THREEFOLD BLESSING OF LOVE, WISDOM AND UNDERSTANDING BE YOURS.

Kisses child and gives to mother.

The Warrior Maid

Being a professional woman (a Warrior Maid) does not preclude being feminine. Wearing a severely-tailored suit and a man's shirt and tie does not make you 'one of the boys'. Neither does it make you vulnerable to wear a pretty and flattering outfit to the office. What does make you vulnerable is the way you think of yourself. How you behave towards others, how you interact with them, and what makes you *strong* is exactly the same thing.

Why should you not wear things that make you, as a person, feel good? A Warrior Maid needs well-cut and flattering 'armour', your very strength is your woman's power, your inner level of creativity and the ability to hold on when a man would have long given up.

However professional you may become, there is still, at the core of your being, a *woman*. But, the cut and thrust of your working day may begin to cover up that core with layer after layer of defensive behaviour. The following ritual may help.

You will need a full Moon, a quiet place out of doors, and some like-minded women (you can do this on your own with some adaptation, but in this day and age a woman alone in a quiet, remote place is asking for trouble. Better to have the protection of a group), plain white robes (they can be made from old sheets, sleeveless, if possible off one shoulder, and to the knee with a slit to the thigh on both sides. Any jewellery should be silver), as big a bowl of grapes as you can afford, red wine (IMPORTANT – those who are driving must make do with red grape juice), cups for the wine (not glass, it is too easy to break them, leaving shards around to cut children and animals), some small bowls, a pair of small nail scissors, a large packet of white chocolate buttons, some diced chicory, some charcoal, incense, a burner and nine white candles. Each woman should have or make a 2–3 foot staff decorated with ribbons, shells, stones, crystals, etc. It should, if possible, have at least one fir cone hanging from it.

Other essentials are taped music (use something rousing and blatant like *The Ritual Fire Dance* – *El Amor Brujo* by De Falla – or slow and sultry like Ravel's *Bolero*. You might prefer something like *The Polotsvian Dances* by Borodin, and Flamenco or Gypsy music, plus any 'danceable' music – you will no doubt have your favourite). Any other food should be 'white' Moon food: chicken, eggs, celery, white cheese, houmus, coleslaw, any fruit, and anything made with almonds. Coronets of ivy and leaves with small white flowers should entwined in the greenery.

Bind your hair close with silver ribbons at the beginning, and wrap yourselves in dark shawls. Wear well-fitting sandals or lightweight white trainers. (If it is a warm night, you might like to take sleeping bags/tents and stay the night.)

When you get to your destination, prepare a small altar; this might be a box or small folding table with a white cloth over it, even better is a rock or stone at the scene. Place a large chalice full of wine in the centre and wind greenery all about it. Lay out the food on the 'green' cloth. Change into your robes and if possible you should be starclad beneath them. If some of you are menstruating, remember that you will be at the height of your powers now. If it is possible and permissible, light a small fire but be careful that it is safely contained. If it takes place in summer there may have been little or no rainfall and a blaze is easily started.

Begin by invoking Diana/Artemis. There should be one high priestess and two to assist her. You could have three to open the ritual and another three to close it. This gives more people something to do and evens out the work. The high priestess stands before the altar with a lighted taper, her handmaids behind and to either side of her. One carries a full bowl of white chocolate broken up into pieces, the other has a bowl of diced chicory. All gather round and link their arms about each other's waists, and begin to sway from side to side. The high priestess begins by holding up her arms to the moon in supplication. (IT IS IMPORTANT THAT THE WORDS ARE LEARNED BY HEART)

High Priestess: I OPEN THE CIRCLE WITH FIRE (circles with incense). I OPEN THE CIRCLE WITH WATER (circles sprinkling water). I OPEN THE CIRCLE WITH EARTH (circles casting salt). I OPEN THE CIRCLE WITH AIR (circles with Fan).

HAIL THOU CHASTE AND FLEET-FOOTED DAUGHTER OF ZEUS, WE OFFER THEE THINGS BITTER AND THINGS SWEET AS DID OUR ANCESTRESSES OF OLD. HAIL, THOU THREE-FACED ONE. (Lights three candles on left side of altar.) HAIL, THOU HUNTRESS OF THE NIGHT. (Lights three candles to right of altar.) HAIL, LADY OF THE BEAR.

(Lights three candles in front of altar.)

Incidentally, the bear was one of Diana's symbols and her priestesses were known as 'little bears'.

First Priestess: I OFFER THE BITTER TASTE OF CHICORY THAT IS THE DARK SIDE OF THE MOON. LET ALL WHO EAT KNOW AND UNDERSTAND THAT TO STAND ALONE CAN BE AT TIMES AS BITTER AS THIS. (Places bowl on the altar, then returns to place and kneels facing altar.)

Second Priestess: I OFFER THE SWEET TASTE OF MILK WHITE CHOCOLATE THAT IS LIKE THE FULL MOON HERSELF. LET ALL WHO EAT KNOW AND UNDERSTAND THAT TO STAND ALONE CAN BE AS SWEET AND AS NOURISHING AS THIS. (Places bowl on altar then returns and kneels facing altar.)

High Priestess: (kneels) OH DIANA OF THE BEASTS, GREAT IS THY NAME AMONG US, TEACH US THY SECRET OF HAPPINESS AND INNER STRENGTH, GIVE US THY BLESSING, MOON GODDESS, THAT WE MAY KNOW THEE MORE FULLY IN THE DANCE AND IN THE SONG, IN THE WINE AND IN THE GRAPE. BIND US TO THEE, AS WE BIND THE LOCK AND THE TRESS. THEN, WHEN THE TIME IS RIGHT SET US FREE WITH UNBOUND HAIR, LIGHT FEET, AND A LIGHT HEART TO DANCE BENEATH THY RADIANT LIGHT.

All rise and join like the others so they are in the centre of the ring, all sway from side to side, singing.

ISIS, ASTARTE, DIANA, HEKATE, DEMETER, KALI, INANNA.[2] (Keep repeating, swelling louder and then dying away.)

High Priestess: SISTERS LET US DANCE UP THE CONE OF POWER.

All join hands and begin to dance in a circle to any music of their choice. As each tape comes to an end, it must be changed so that the dance is continuous, but always in a circle and as far as possible hand in hand. When all are totally exhausted, end the dance, and let them eat and drink. As they do this each woman in turn goes up to the altar and offers a drop of wine from her glass, and a small piece of whatever she is eating. They each offer a prayer of their own devising, asking for whatever they wish to receive from the Virgin Goddess.

Now the bowl of grapes is brought and handed around for all to eat. At this point put on something slow and erotic like *The Ritual Fire Dance*. As she feels called, let each woman get up and dance by herself, offering the energy of her dance to Diana. The music may be changed from the slow to the fiery. Finally all stand and unbind their hair, shaking it free, then they pick up their staffs and put them in the middle of the circle and begin the ISIS, ASTARTE, DIANA, HEKATE, DEMETER, KALI, INANNA chant. Begin to circle, getting faster and faster, keeping up the chant. Now break the circle, pick up your staffs and run, run wherever you like, for as far as you need, like the Bacchantes of old. Thresh about you with the staffs, leaping and dancing, rolling on the grass and always singing the names of the Goddess. When you have had enough return to the altar and sit in a semi-circle in front of it. Rest quietly for a while, then the high priestess and her two handmaids come to the altar.

High Priestess: GRACIOUS LADY, LOVELY MAIDEN, WISE ONE, WE ASK YOU TO LOOK UPON THOSE GATHERED HERE TO PRAISE YOU WITH SONG AND DANCE, WITH WINE AND GRAPE. NOW WE SEEK YOUR GENTLE SIDE, THE SIDE OF THE GIVER OF DREAMS. THE WARRIOR MAID WITH HER QUIVER OF SILVER ARROWS AND HER BOW OF THE CRESCENT MOON IS LAID ASIDE. WE SEEK PERSEPHONE, WE SEEK ATHENE THE WEAVER, WE SEEK THE TITANESS WITHIN EACH OF US THAT WE MAY BE STRONG WITHOUT DESTROYING, STAND FAST WITHOUT BECOMING INFLEXIBLE. KEEP US TRUE TO OUR WOMANHOOD AND THE FOUNT OF WISDOM THAT LIES WITHIN EACH GIRL CHILD AT BIRTH AND GROWS WITH HER.

She picks up the empty bowl and goes around circle, each woman placing a few hairs from her head in the bowl. Meanwhile one of the handmaids lights new charcoal and burns fresh incense. The hair is brought to the altar and the high priestess and her attendants add their hair. Then it is placed bit by bit on the burning incense until all is gone.

First Priestess: LADY OF THE NIGHT SKY, KEEPER OF THE EVENING STAR, SET YOUR FOOT ON THE EARTH THIS NIGHT AND SPILL YOUR LIGHT ON US. KEEP US

MINDFUL OF OUR SISTERS IN OTHER LANDS, OTHER RACES AND BELIEFS, LET US FULLY UNDERSTAND OUR SISTERHOOD EXTENDS BEYOND THE EARTH INTO THE REALMS OF THE INFINITE.

She takes the empty bowl and the nail scissors and goes around the circle. Each women gives a nail paring, dropping it into the bowl. Then it is taken to the altar and the others add their token. This is now taken to the fire and all thrown in together.

THUS DO WE GIVE PART OF OURSELVES TO BE MINGLED IN THE FIRE OF FELLOWSHIP.

Second Priestess: THOU SILVER-HAIRED WISE ONE, BRINGER IN OF DEATH, MIDWIFE OF THE SOUL, GUARD US IN OUR SLEEP, AND WHEN WE SLEEP THE LAST SLEEP OF ALL HOLD US IN YOUR ARMS AND CARRY US BEYOND THE RISING MOON TO A PLACE OF PEACE.

She takes the Chalice and carries it round for all to share, returns to the altar and pours what is left on to the earth.

WHAT GREW FROM THE EARTH I RETURN TO THE EARTH WITH OUR LOVE FOR THE GRACE AND STRENGTH OF GAIA THE MOTHER.

High Priestess: I CLOSE UP THE CIRCLE WITH FIRE (takes around the censer), I CLOSE UP THE CIRCLE WITH WATER (sprinkles water around circle), I CLOSE UP THE CIRCLE WITH EARTH (sprinkles circle with salt), I CLOSE UP THE CIRCLE WITH AIR (goes around with fan of feathers). ALL IS DONE.

Clear up, make it all tidy, leave no litter, depart quietly. If you are camping overnight, get to sleep as soon as you can. Record any dreams that come.

Losing Love

Nothing is worse than feeling yourself bound by thoughts, energies and memories to a love that has gone sour and died. You may no longer love someone but his image seems to be constantly before you, everything reminds you of the time you spent together. Even a legal separation or divorce which may cut legal ties does not always cut the emotional ones.

The trouble is with the subconscious mind. Legal documents mean nothing to it, it cannot read. It came into being when humankind was very young, it understands only images, symbols, pictures. That is why even now a symbol like a little lion on an egg, a lion in football shorts and shirt, or something as simple as five circles entwined as in the Olympic flag can cause an emotion or a recognition signal to rise up within us.

In order to convince one's subconscious that a marriage or a love affair is over and done with, you are going to have to do it by symbolic actions and pictures. Did you know that most divorcees throw their weddings rings into a river or the sea? It is a symbolic act, albeit most of the time an unknowing one. Water washes things away, it is symbol of new life, a new wave of energy sweeping through one. A strong wind will do much the same thing. You can cut away from your old life in many ways. Some of them seem a little ridiculous.

1 You can dress up (from the skin out) in clothes that you bought/wore when you were with your old love. Wear them all day and keep telling yourself that they are a symbol of the old, and very dead, times. In the evening, go upstairs with a large black plastic bag. Run a bath with some nice bath oil, (please do not use rosemary, as it is for remembrance!!!) Open the plastic bag and stand on it. Then carefully undress so that each garment does not touch the floor but drops into the bag. When you are naked step off the plastic and tie it off with all the clothing inside. Step into the bath and have a good long soak to get all traces of the clothing off your body. Wash your hair thoroughly, do your nails. Then dry yourself with a *new* towel and put on a *new* nightdress and go to bed between *new* sheets. In the morning put the clothing in the dustbin. *Do not* take it to Oxfam or the jumble, someone else will pick up your sorrows. Let it go into the earth and rot away.

2 Get a balloon and stretch the neck until you can insert the pieces of a torn-up photo of your 'ex'. Fill the balloon with helium, or just air, let it go from the top of a cliff overlooking the sea, or on a high hill. Attach it to a kite and let it out to the end of its string, then let go. Helium is best because it will simply go up until it bursts.

3 Go swimming in the sea and take with you a plastic bag of mementos from your past life. Empty them when you are

as far out as is safe for you. Alternatively, take a ferry ride –
maybe a day trip to France – and drop them overboard. The
subconscious mind will take note of this and accept that it
is now in the past.

However, you can also do the job by ritual, using the Four
Elements and the power of the Moon. You will need a ball of
red wool, a bowl of water, some twigs, paper and a firelighter,
a small spade or trowel, a rose, and a small thurible full of
burning incense. You will also need four small pictures of your
former partner, or four small articles that belonged to him, or
a mixture of both, some matches, a mirror, a small phial of
perfume, a sea shell, a little bell on a ribbon and a pair of
scissors or a sharp knife.

You need a quiet space where you will not be disturbed, if
it can be near the sea, a river, or a lake so much the better.
It should be done at the full of the Moon so that when it begins
to wane it will take all the pain and bad memories out of your
life. It is more powerful if done actually under the full Moon.
Cut two twelve-foot lengths of the wool and place them in an
equal-armed cross orientated with the four directions. In the
East, at the farthest end of the wool, place the thurible and
one of the pictures. In the South place the dry wood, paper
and firelighter and another picture. In the West put the bowl
of water and a third picture. In the North dig a hole about nine
or ten inches deep and put the rose beside it, and the last
picture. The rose must carry on its petals a trace of your
vaginal fluids.

Take your place where the two lengths cross. Sit down and
meditate on your past life and why you are here and what you
intend to do. Relax, slow down your breathing, centre your
mind and your consciousness on the moment.

Summon to mind the image of your ex-partner and, no
matter how acrimonious the parting has been, *do not* at any
point of the ritual wish him harm. To do so might well bring
what you wish him back on yourself.

Begin, facing East.

MOON MOTHER, I GREET YOU IN YOUR FULLNESS
AND OFFER THE GIFT OF A MIRROR IN WHICH YOU MAY
SEE YOUR FACE. (Lay mirror down to catch the reflection if

possible) I ASK FOR HELP IN CUTTING ANY TIES THAT
MAY STILL EXIST BETWEEN MY FORMER PARTNER AND
MYSELF. I DO NOT SEEK TO HARM OR CAUSE PAIN,
ONLY FREEDOM FROM THE TIES THAT ONCE BOUND US
TOGETHER.

I LOOK TOWARDS THE EAST AND IN MY MEMORIES
I SEE A TIME WHEN WE WERE HAPPY TOGETHER. THAT
TIME HAS PAST AND I WISH TO CUT IT AWAY SO THAT
WE MAY BOTH BE FREE. THE SMOKE OF THE INCENSE
RISES AND DISPERSES INTO THE AIR. IN THE SAME WAY
I WISH THE PAST REPRESENTED BY THE PICTURE TO
TRANSMUTE INTO SCENTED SMOKE AND BE TAKEN BY
THE WIND OVER THE HILLS AND FAR AWAY. I WISH YOU
WELL (his name) BUT I SET US BOTH FREE IN THE
DIRECTION OF THE EAST AND BY THE POWER OF THE
MOON.

Get up and take the photo, place it on the smouldering
incense grains and allow it to turn to ash, cut the red cord
about six inches from the thurible, and return to your place.

AS I HAVE ASKED, SO MAY IT BE THIS NIGHT, BLESSED
BY THE POWER OF THE MOON. NOW I TURN MY FACE
TO THE SOUTH AND I GREET YOU MOON MOTHER,
AND I OFFER THE GIFT OF PERFUME TO PLEASE YOU.
(pour phial of perfume over ground) AGAIN I ASK FOR
YOUR HELP IN SETTING MYSELF FREE FROM THE PAST.
I ASK THAT OUR FUTURE PATHS MAY BE FILLED WITH
LIGHT AND WARMTH OF HEART.

AS I LOOK IN THE DIRECTION OF THE SOUTH I
REMEMBER A TIME WHEN WE MADE LOVE AND THE
HEAT OF PASSION CAME TO LIFE WITHIN US. NOW
THAT TIME IS PAST AND THE FIRE IS DEAD. I WILL
LIGHT ANOTHER FIRE, THE FIRE OF CLEANSING FLAME
AND BY ITS POWER THE ASHES OF OUR FORGOTTEN
LOVE WILL BE SCATTERED TO THE WINDS TO BE TAKEN
WHERE THEY WILL. I SET US BOTH FREE IN THE
DIRECTION OF THE SOUTH AND BY THE POWER OF THE
MOON.

Get up and light small fire, place photo on it and let it burn
away to ashes. When cold after the rite, scatter them well. Cut
the cord six inches from the fire and return to your place.

AS I HAVE ASKED SO MAY IT BE THIS NIGHT, BLESSED

BY THE POWER OF THE MOON.

NOW I TURN MY FACE TO THE WEST AND I GREET YOU MOON MOTHER, AND I OFFER A SEA SHELL FOR YOUR DELIGHT. FOR THE THIRD TIME I ASK FOR YOUR HELP IN CUTTING MY TIES WITH THE PAST. I ASK THAT BOTH OF US MAY FIND LOVE AGAIN IN THE DAYS TO COME. I LOOK WEST AND REMEMBER A MOMENT WHEN WE DRANK TOGETHER AND MADE A TOAST TO THE FUTURE. THAT FUTURE NEVER MANIFESTED. I WILL SCATTER THE PIECES OF MY MEMORIES INTO THE WATERS OF THE MOON AND WASH AWAY MY TEARS.

Go to the bowl of water, tear up the photo and throw it into the bowl. This will be thrown into a larger body of water after the ritual. Cut the cord and return to your place as before.

NOW I TURN MY FACE TO THE NORTH AND I GREET YOU MOON MOTHER. I OFFER A BELL ON A RIBBON FOR YOUR PLEASURE. FOR THE LAST TIME I ASK FOR YOUR HELP IN LEAVING THE PAST BEHIND. I ASK FOR UNDERSTANDING AND WISDOM TO BE GIVEN TO US BOTH. AS I LOOK TO THE NORTH I REMEMBER WHEN WE ATE TOGETHER THE FRUITS OF THE EARTH AND WERE HAPPY. THAT TIME NO LONGER APPLIES TO US. I WILL FINALLY BURY THE ROSE OF LOVE AND COVER IT WITH THE IMAGE OF MY FORMER LOVER. THE EARTH WILL TAKE BOTH SYMBOLS BACK INTO ITSELF AND SET US FREE IN THE DIRECTION OF THE NORTH AND BY THE POWER OF THE MOON.

Get up and go to the North, place the rose in the hole and the photo on top, sprinkle some flower seeds if you wish, then cover it up with earth. Cut the cord and return to your place.

AS I HAVE ASKED SO MAY IT BE THIS NIGHT BLESSED BY THE POWER OF THE MOON.

Remain in meditation for a few minutes. Then get up and bow three times to the Moon. Scatter the ashes from the fire and the thurible. If there is water near you throw the bowl of water and its contents into it, if not then water the roots of a bush with it and lightly cover the torn scraps with earth. Place the mirror where it catches the Moon's face, leave the shell in open ground and tie the bell to the branch of a tree. Collect all the pieces of red cord and bury them.

Notes

1 The tape on which these meditations can be heard is available from:
SOL,
PO Box 215,
St Helier,
Jersey,
CI, UK,
price £5.50 (plus 50p postage and packing).
2 The tune to this chant can be found on many New Age Wiccan Tapes. Best known is *Catch the Fire* by Charlie Murphy.

PART 4
AUTUMN
Harvest Time

10

THE LAST FLOWING

Time To Start Living

When your last period passes it leaves something of a gap in your life. You have been so used to its arrival and all that it entails that it has become an integral part of your life, accepted as if it will go on forever. But it doesn't.

Some women who hate it all their lives, who cannot see the beauty and the power in it, will be glad to see it pass forever from their lives. Others will sorrow for it as something that will never be the same. Often there is a feeling of depression akin to that which sometimes afflicts young mothers after childbirth.

More and more women are seeing their periods continue later in life – up to one's late-fifties is not uncommon. Many women go on to HRT or Hormonal Replacement Therapy as soon as the menopause occurs. It does have some very good effects, keeping the skin supple and young-looking, helping with things like bone loss, etc. It can, however, have an effect on your weight if you have problems with obesity, and of course it does mean you will continue to have a blood loss each month. A talk with your doctor is needed to sort out any problems you may have.

The menopause itself can often give rise to health problems – women need to take care of themselves a little more; exercise and diet should be looked at carefully. However, there is no need to suppose that you will lose anything of your femininity, your attractiveness, or your enjoyment of sex. Thorsons have a whole selection of books dealing with female problems, along with others on diet and mental outlook on this time of life.

For some women menstruation will simply stop, and never come again. For others it will cease gradually, and may stop for a while then reappear. For some it is a time of agitation and worry, of headaches and various ills, most of which are psychosomatic. Yet others sail through it with little or no problems. It can become an excuse for behaviour patterns or it can begin a new, wonderful, and extremely powerful phase of your life. The choice, as always, is yours.

In the mysteries there is a time, a place and a working for all experiences. When you were little and celebrated your birthdays you may have been measured against the doorpost as each party day came round. Remember how excited you were when you saw the new mark being made. Remember how people greeted you with 'My, how you have grown'. This new phase is part of the same kind of growing except that you are growing inwardly instead of upwards.

Your life is not to be seen as being nearly over, but as the start of a new beginning. You have reached a time when you are to be seen as an elder. As a person who understands responsibility and who can take charge, who is looked up to, and sought out for advice. You have a valuable commodity to offer to family, friends and the community, you have 'hands on' experience.

All too often as you approach that certain time in a woman's life you can begin to feel as if you are no longer useful, no longer attractive. The wolf whistles from the building sites are no longer for you! Well, turn the tables, it is about time you gave the wolf whistles . . . What? you wouldn't dare? Why not? Do you think you are too old to enjoy a pair of broad shoulders, rippling muscles and a pair of tight jeans? Let me tell you Grandma, this is a terrific time of life, you can do the things younger women wouldn't dare. They are all so busy being liberated and 'free', that they are missing out on all the fun. Let the feminists look down their noses as an admiring male looks at their legs. It can do the male ego a power of good when an older and obviously appreciative woman gives *them* a speculative look.

Hell, woman, go out and get what you want, you have earned it, you can appreciate it, and you know what to do with it!

Do you want to start your own business? Why not? Do you

want to travel? Why not? I do, some 60/70,000 miles a year, sometimes alone, sometimes with my daughter who is also my best pal and sometimes with my 90-year-old mother who still lectures, and could give Madonna lessons in how to enchant the opposite sex. Christine Hartley, before she died in her late 80s, was one of the most beautiful women I have known. Waiters hurried to get her a chair, offer her coffee, or call her a taxi, she would give them her special 1,000-watt smile and they lit up like Christmas trees. *You*, Daughter of Eve, have nothing to prove, you have it all.

If you are married it is time to think about a second honeymoon. If you are a widow, it is time to save up and go on a cruise to some exciting new place. Who knows, there may be someone of your own age thinking about doing the same thing. So your family may say things like, 'What *are* you thinking of, and at *your* age', or 'Mother, I really don't think you should go all that way on your own'. Explain to them, forcibly if that is what it takes, that you have taken care of them for most of their lives and done a good job. You are certainly old enough now to look after yourself. Most of the time they are plain jealous.

Coffee mornings, organising jumble sales and the annual church fete may satisfy some, but there is still fresh, green grass on the other side of the hill.

Have you seen the television programme called *The Golden Girls*? Well, that is what you should be looking for now. Just because you no longer menstruate, or because you now collect a pension, there is no reason to start thinking in terms of sheltered housing and wheelchairs.

There are gyms and health centres in almost every city and town nowadays. They often have reduced subscriptions for older people. Swimming pools sometimes offer not only reduced fees but have special days or times that are specially for older people and you can swim without being bombarded by youngsters, or hassled by would-be Olympic medalists. Swimming is one of the best forms of exercises you can have, it supports you and yet makes you use almost every muscle in your body.

Age is not a matter of years, Daughter of Eve, it is a matter of the way you think. If you think of yourself as being old and past it, then that is the image you will project to other people.

In terms of the mysteries you are now into the time of *The Crone*. In the old days this was usually depicted by a traditional witch type, looking like a model for a Grimm's fairy tale. Today's Crone, however, is a smart, well-dressed, well-informed and outgoing woman, fully conscious of herself as a valuable member of society. This is one of your most important Rites of Passage. It is not a defeat, it is a victory. Remember that in the burning times of the Middle Ages, very few women of our kind lived to become a Crone.

If ever you go on a cruise, look around you, you will find a good proportion of your companions on board ship are either retired or coming up to retirement. People, especially women, are living much longer and maintaining their health, both mentally and physically. By the end of this century it will no longer be a rarity for human beings to see one hundred years, and even more. But longer years are not all that is needed for quality of life, the ability to feel a useful part of one's family is also a bonus.

The Time of the Crone may be one that comes with the riper years, but a Crone by the very nature of her calling is a Wise Woman, wise for herself as well as others. When there is nothing to stimulate the mind, then the mind will fall in upon itself like a failing wall. It is your duty to teach, train and prepare others to take your place. The mothers of older children are the women who will, in another decade or so, be ready to take on the part of the Wise Woman, and without you they will not have the knowledge they will need.

The traditional wisdom, the 'old wive's tales' if you like, the old stories and ways of doing things, the games and songs and nursery rhymes, all these would die out of it were not for the Crones. Your Last Flowing closed the door on your role as a Giver of Life, but it opened a window to a new one as a Teller of Tales, a Keeper of Traditions, as a Wise Woman.

Fill your days with laughter and study, with service and with conversation, discussions, arguments and disagreements. Read, not only the daily papers, but the more challenging magazines. There is bound to be one with something that interests you. Perhaps you were, in your younger days, a Warrior Maid, perhaps there is no family of your own to spoil and take on outings. There are many young families that have no older woman to turn to, young people who, for one reason or another, were brought up as orphans or who lost their parents young. Their children need grandmothers, stories told at bedtime, a little spoiling now and then; someone to help decorate a Christmas tree or help unwrap parcels on Christmas morning. A volunteer granny can bring a lot of happiness to both parts.

Whatever you do, don't sit and mope. For years you have had to cook clean, wash, mend, put plasters on cuts and soothe fears and tantrums. Now things are going to be different. It's your world out there, go and grab it by its ears.

11

THE EMPTY HOUSE

The Widow

Sometimes, life's circumstances take away those that you love. To lose a loved and loving partner after many years of marriage can be devastating. If there has been a long illness, the strain of nursing and watching your partner gradually slip away, of long nights with little sleep, is bound to take its toll of your strength. This is the time to call on your right as a Crone to invoke the greatest power of the Goddess. You have the right to ask for the Grace of the Second Road. If the one you love is suffering, if no hope can be given to you, then you may call on the Goddess to open the Second Road to him. But, as always, it must be Her decision.

I have included in the rituals for this part of the book one called The Vigil, and one that will show you how to ask for 'Crone Right', as well as the Last Flowing, and some others. You should realise that simply being a Crone enhances your psychic powers in a new and different way. One of them is the power of the Priestess of the Dead and Dying. In the past it was always the older women to whom families turned for instruction on the care of the sick and the laying out of the dead. Nowadays it is all done for us, but if you wish to do it, it is your right.

The feel of a house that once echoed to the laughter of your children and your partner and which is now silent and empty can be demoralising. There is nothing so empty as an empty house. Often older people find it hard to give up a house in which they have spent much of their life and which has seen joys and sorrows, births and marriages, and so many happy times. If you can bear to leave it can be much better for you – cutting the ties makes a new life without someone beside you easier. Not so much room, not so many familiar things. Yes, it is a wrench to leave the house you loved, but it means that another family can bask in the warmth that you have built into it over the years.

Much as you have loved, please do not think that you can never love again. Sometimes, companionship can be a blessing even if the fire and the passion of what you knew long ago are not there. All experiences that make us pause and look back can be classed as Rites of Passage. The one that is often the hardest to bear is the leaving of a home in which you have been happy. There is something about closing a door and handing the key to a stranger that is very final. It happens even in younger times when you move to a new place. You find yourself 'accidentally passing by' and looking at the new curtains and the new plants in the garden. It is part of human nature.

The learning experiences of the Crone are those of giving up and giving away. You must learn the art of balance, to live with joy and look forward to years with your grandchildren growing up. To seeing new places and doing new things, and the realisation that this is Harvest time and you are the corn being cut down and made into sheaves. This will ultimately become the bread of experience that will feed others. No one lives in vain, no matter how long, how short, how steeped in sorrow or rich in joy, there is always something, even one thing, that makes it all worthwhile. We grow as we live. Each day a little more is added to our understanding of the world around us and our effect upon it.

The Empty Nest

There are other reasons for an empty nest. Every mother of a bride knows how it feels when they finally get home after the wedding, put the kettle on and kick off the shoes that have been killing them all day. You sink down into the armchair, sip your tea and pause . . . the house is quiet. There is no sound, no high decibel levels of Bruce Springsteen, no honey-thick tones of Lionel Richie, no frantic pipings from Prince, just silence. If you look around you will see the odd mound of confetti, a pair of discarded white stockings, empty sherry glasses and half-eaten canapes, but it will be empty. The little bride has flown. Of course, upstairs her room is a mess but for the first time you won't mind cleaning it up.

Do you know what you should do, Daughter of Eve, the morning after the last child has flown the nest? Go down to the nearest travel agent and book yourself a holiday, even if it is only a couple of days in the country. It will be the first time you have been on your own since they were born. Why should the bride and groom be the only ones on honeymoon.

Now is the time to think about turning the spare bedroom into a study and writing that book you have had in mind for years. This is your chance to take on that night school course, learn a language, take up origami, or self defence. What about the Open University and a degree? That is just as valid as a Rite of Passage. For the first time for years you can do what you want without thinking about babysitters, new shoes for the children, and PTA meetings.

Looking Back

All human beings need to look back, they need to recap on their lives from time to time. For a woman each area of her life is quite distinct. Childhood, girlhood, teenage and the first period, and then woman. Bride and mother leading on to mother of the bride, grandmother and now the menopause. It can come as a shock to realise that you can never have another baby. You may not have wanted another one, but even if you did, now it is too late. That fact alone can make a woman feel very strange. The first child is a wonder, the last one is a bitter-sweet experience, but now there will be no more. That, Daughter of Eve, is a bitter Rite of Passage, and yet out of it can come this enormous freedom, your reward for all the times when you have given your self, your time, your love and your strength to your family. Look back, not in anger, but in pride.

In all those years, since this book began with your

childhood, you have been growing towards something. As you passed through each new phase of your life there was something ahead of you. At that time it was always with someone else in mind – your lover, your husband, your children – now everything ahead is for *you*.

For a moment let me turn the clock back to a time when you are, say, in your twenties. This is the time to take out an insurance policy, it need not be a very big one, just one that will, when you have reached the autumn years, enable you to do something you have always wanted to do. It might be a trip to South America to see the Andes, or Hawaii. It might be a nose job, or a face lift, it might be a dress from a top-line designer, or a pair of diamond stud earrings. Whatever it is, go for it. There are two places on this earth that I have longed to see since I was old enough to look at and understand my father's big atlas. One is the Magellan Straits, between Chile and Tierra Del Fuego, the other location is the Aleutian Islands off Alaska. It is now 1992 as I write, and in 1993 I am off . . . to one of those two places. Which one? Well, I shall have to think about that.

12

THE RITUALS

The Last Flowing
Of course it will not be possible to predict any kind of date
for your last menstruation, but what you can do is wait until
you have not had a period for at least six months, check with
your doctor to make sure all is well, then accept that you have
entered the exciting time of your Cronehood. This ritual is a
Rite of Passage but it can be worked in combination with the
following rite which is a thanksgiving for any children you
may have had, for a safe and healthy passage through the time
of your menses.

If circumstances, or a medical condition, have meant the
removal of the womb, this ritual can be performed ahead of
time. However, remember that there is an astral counterpart
of everything, including body organs. This is why people who
have had a limb amputated can still 'feel' it, can still wiggle
fingers and toes of the non-existent limb. Astrally, you still
have a womb. You can get in touch with me through the school
address at the back of this book – so long as we have a group
working within a reasonable distance of you, I will do my best
to arrange a Reconsecration of the Womb ceremony. We have
quite a few groups now, worldwide, headed by competent and
caring women who will perform this important ritual.

If your life has been concerned with the mysteries then you
will have women friends who will happily join you and work
with you. If you are a solitary worker then it can easily be adapted.

If it is not possible for a woman to gather others about her
for this ceremony, it can be done as a silent pathworking
within the mind. Summon the angelic powers about you and
pass the various symbols of power to them.

You might like to record the words and listen to them as you build the images in your mind. Remember that mental ritual work is as valid and as powerful as that performed on the physical level.

First, prepare ahead of time by placing a bowl of water under the first light of a new moon and every night after that up to the night before the full moon, to charge up with lunar power. Purchase a Cowrie shell to represent the female part of yourself. The rite itself will take place on the night of the full moon. You will need a small table with a white cloth for an altar. On the table, place a centre light (a nightlight in a red bowl is apt), a red flower and a white flower, a red candle and a white candle, a chalice of red wine, some moon cakes (almond flavoured), a red cord to wear about your waist over your robe, and a silver one to put on the altar for later.

During the preceding months, while you have been waiting for the right time, you will have been making a special wand. Take a piece of wood a small branch from a tree (for full instructions on making a wand see *The Ritual Magic Workbook*). Dry it and smooth it, then varnish it with clear varnish. Cut a notch at one end and wedge into it a piece of silver. This might be a charm, a coin, or a piece of silver wire from a jeweller. Wind a red silk thread from the notch round and down, adding a tiny spot of glue at intervals to keep it in place. Fasten it in the same way at the bottom and wind another piece of silver wire around the wand at the base. The silver at the top will symbolise your First Flowing; the winding spiral of red silk your menses through the years; and the silver at the base the Last Flowing. This is placed on the altar.

Prepare a little supper and ask your friends to each bring something for the feast, perhaps a bottle of wine or a cake, etc. It is important to invite among them a younger woman to whom you feel you can pass on the wand you have made.

Ask your friends to arrive at moonrise and welcome them in with a kiss and a silver coin – an English five pence piece or an American ten cent piece, or anything small and silvery. It symbolises a little piece of the Moon given in love and friendship.

When everyone has arrived call them together, seat them around the altar and light the centre light. Ask one of them to take the part of the Moon Mother. Do not speak of your choice with regard to the giving of the wand, let that be a secret until the time comes.

The Moon Mother stands in the West by the chalice, you stand in the East with your wand. The Moon Bowl is also in the West, with a small amount of sea salt in a salt cellar, the two candles are either side of the centre light, the moon cakes are in the north, and the Cowrie shell is in the south. The silver cord lies across the altar from East to West. The red cord you are wearing. The Moon Mother lights the red and white candles from the centre light and dips the Cowrie shell into the wine so that it holds a little of it within the shell itself. This represents your last flowing.

Moon Mother: THIS IS THE ALTAR OF THE MOON, I SPRINKLE IT WITH SEA SALT TO CLEANSE IT AND WITH WATER FROM THE MOON BOWL TO HALLOW AND BLESS IT. IN THE SACRED NAMES OF SELENE AND DIANA, OF CELEMON AND HECATE, I BLESS THIS ALTAR AND THIS GATHERING. DAUGHTER OF THE MOON, WHY HAVE YOU CALLED YOUR SISTERS TOGETHER AND SET UP THE ALTAR OF THE MOON?

Crone: THAT I MAY PASS THROUGH THE RITE OF PASSAGE TO MY CRONEHOOD AND CLAIM THE POWER THAT IS MY RIGHT. THIS I CAN ONLY DO THROUGH THE POWER OF THE MOON.

Moon Mother: TO CLAIM THE POWER OF THE CRONE YOU MUST GIVE UP THAT WHICH IS THE POWER OF THE MOTHER. THE FLOWING MUST CEASE AND ITS POWERS BE PASSED ON TO ANOTHER. ONCE GIVEN THERE IS NO TURNING BACK IN THIS LIFE. THE POWER TO GIVE LIFE WILL BE TAKEN FROM YOU, BUT THE TWIN POWERS OF UNDERSTANDING AND WISDOM WILL BE YOURS, AS WILL THE POWER OF CRONE RIGHT TO CALL THE GENTLE ANGEL OF DEATH TO THOSE WHOSE TIME IS NEAR. ARE YOU READY AND WILLING TO PASS THE POWERS YOU HAVE NOW TO ANOTHER, AND TO STAND BEREFT OF POWER BEFORE ME, TRUSTING IN THE LAW OF THE MOON THAT ANOTHER DOOR WILL OPEN TO YOU THIS NIGHT?

Crone: I WILL GIVE UP MY POWERS OF THE FLOWING TO TAKE ON THOSE OF THE CRONE. I WILL PASS THOSE

POWERS TO ANOTHER WITHOUT REGRET. I AM
WILLING TO STAND BEFORE THE MOON MOTHER
BEREFT OF POWER AND WAIT FOR HER WILL TO GRANT
ME CRONE RIGHT OR NO. SO MOTE IT BE.

Moon Mother: I LIGHT THE RED CANDLE, SYMBOL OF
THE FLOWING, TO ACTIVATE THE LAST OF ITS POWERS
WITHIN YOU. (gives candle to crone) LOOK ON ITS FLAME,
FOR WITH ITS GIVING THE FORCE OF LIFE WILL DIE
WITHIN YOU.

Crone meditates upon the flame for a minute or two, then
circles the group of women, finally choosing one of the
younger women and passing the lighted candle to her, then
returns to altar.

Crone: I HAVE PASSED THE FLAME OF THE FLOWING
OF LIFE ON TO ANOTHER. WHAT ELSE MUST I DO NOW
MOON MOTHER?

Moon Mother: ANOTHER CHANCE I GIVE TO THEE, THE
WAND OF THE MOTHER POWERS IS TO YOUR HAND.
WITH IT YOU MAY CALL BACK THE POWERS YOU GAVE
AWAY. IF YOU GIVE IT, THOSE POWERS WILL GO WITH
THE GIFT, NEVER TO RETURN. ARE YOU READY AND
WILLING TO GIVE THOSE POWERS?

Crone: I AM READY AND WILLING TO PASS THEM ON
TO ANOTHER. NOR WILL I ASK FOR THEM TO BE
RETURNED. SO MOTE IT BE.

Moon Mother: THEN TAKE THE WAND OF POWER AND
GIVE IT FREELY AND WITH LOVE TO ANOTHER, THEN
RETURN TO ME.

Crone: I HAVE MADE MY CHOICE (she circles the group
once, passes the wand to the woman she has chosen, and
returns to altar) I HAVE DONE AS YOU ASKED, THE WAND
HAS BEEN PASSED TO ANOTHER.

Moon Mother: ONE LAST CHANCE I GIVE THEE TO KEEP
THY POWERS AS THE MOTHER. THE CORD ABOUT
YOUR WAIST IS THE CORD OF BLOOD FLOW, IT CARRIES
THE POWER OF A PRIESTESS OF LIFE. WILL YOU KEEP
IT, OR WILL YOU GIVE IT, NEVER TO HAVE IT AGAIN IN
THIS LIFE?

Crone: I WILL GIVE IT, THE LAST OF ALL MY POWER
SYMBOLS, WILLINGLY AND WITH LOVE. I GIVE ALL UP
THAT I MAY BE WITHOUT POWERS OF ANY KIND.

Moon Mother: THEN GIVE IT, MY DAUGHTER, AND RETURN TO ME.

Crone: THIS IS THE LAST OF MY POWERS. (unties cord, circles group once, then gives cord to her choice and returns to altar)

Moon Mother: DAUGHTER, YOU HAVE GIVEN UP ALL THAT YOU POSSESS AND NOW I TAKE FROM YOU THE LAST FLOWING. (picks up Cowrie shell filled with wine and washes it in the water of the Moon Bowl) THUS I WASH AWAY THE LAST FLOWING AND LEAVE YOU EMPTY OF THE LIFE-GIVING POWERS. BUT WITHIN THE WATERS OF THE MOON BOWL, BY MY POWER AS THE MOON I WILL TRANSMUTE THE LAST FLOWING INTO THE POWERS OF WISDOM AND OF UNDERSTANDING. (takes a little of the water with the shell and drops it into the chalice of wine and blesses it) I AM THE MOON MOTHER AND BY THE POWER OF THE MOON I BLESS THIS CUP, THIS WINE AND WITH THE WINE THIS WOMAN WHO HAS GIVEN ALL SHE HAD, IN THE HOPE OF GIVING EVEN MORE IN SERVICE. DRINK THIS WINE AND IN ITS DRINKING TAKE INTO YOURSELF THE POWERS OF THE CRONE. (gives chalice to crone)

Crone: WITH THIS CUP I PASS THROUGH INTO THE NEW PHASE OF MY LIFE AND MY SERVICE. (holds it up high) BY THE CUP I CLAIM CRONE POWER AND CRONE RIGHT. (drinks it down completely then washes cup in the Moon Bowl)

Moon Mother: THOSE POWERS AND THAT RIGHT IS NOW YOURS. IN TOKEN OF WHICH I GIVE THIS SILVER CORD TO BIND ABOUT YOUR WAIST, THIS WHITE CANDLE (lights candle and gives to her) TO LIGHT YOUR WAY, AND A TASTE OF THE MOON TO MAKE YOUR WORDS GENTLE AND WISE. (gives moon cake) SO MOTE IT BE THIS NIGHT. BLESSED BE THE MOON.

All: BLESSED BE THE MOON AND THE MOON MOTHER. WELCOME TO THE CRONE.

All come to the new-made Crone and wish her well. The Feast may now begin. The water should be poured away on a garden afterwards. The powers given up will continue to wane with the dying Moon, then with the next New Moon the Crone takes up her new powers fully.

Thanksgiving

This can be done by the Crone as a solo working at a time when she is alone and quiet. It is often done as the first ritual *after* attaining her Crone powers.

On the altar you will need a centre light, a scattering of white flower petals, a small bowl of water and salt which have been blessed and mixed, a small plate covered with a white paper napkin and on it a silver Crescent (this can be made out of card and covered with foil, and should be one of four moon symbols that the Crone uses in her kind of magic), a half moon (i.e. half foil and the other half painted with black enamel paint), a full moon, all silver, and a dark moon, all black (make each shape about five to six inches in size), a small bowl of silver coins (five pence pieces would be fine). *If* you can spare three pounds worth you can make it ten pence pieces or even fifty pence pieces. If you can spare more, go up in multiples of three, six, nine pounds, etc, three being the Female power number. The number of the moon is actually nine, but that can be a lot of money to put out.

Buy yourself a large white candle – one that, if left, would burn for at least twenty four hours. Again, if you can afford an even larger one, do it. This candle should be lit for a few minutes at the waning of the moon each month. Why the waning time? Because you have gone through the New Moon phase of your life, the Waxing time, and the Full time, now you are into the Waning time and this is when your Crone power is at its height. In another ten or fifteen years you will work best in the dark of the moon.

This candle can also be used every time you work solo magic. Anointed with good quality oil it will gain in power each time it is used and will last for a long time.

Cleanse your place of working with the salt and water, then at the altar, light the large candle from the smaller centre light. Carry this candle around the circle nine times slowly, laying down a trail of silver light. Set it down safely and make your invocation.

MOON MOTHER, MADE NEW AND YOUNG THIS NIGHT, HEAR THE PRAYER OF THE CRONE.

AN ELDERESS AM I, POWERED BY THE LAST FLOWING.

MISTRESS OF MAGIC AND BELDAME OF THE RITE.

THE NEW MOON IS MY THOUGHT, WAXING DAY BY DAY,

THE FULL MOON IS MY SPELL, CAST TO THE FOUR WINDS,

THE WANING MOON IS MY FULL POWER AS THE CRONE.

IN THE DARK MOON I SHALL MAKE THE FULL CIRCLE.

THE INTENTION OF MY RITE IS A THANKSGIVING FOR MY SAFE AND HEALTHY PASSAGE THROUGH THE TIME OF MAID, WIFE, AND MOTHER (or WARRIOR MAID).

I GIVE THANKS FOR MY MARRIAGE AND FOR MY PARTNER (or, FOR MY SUCCESS AND MY PARTNER),

FOR THE GIFT OF CHILDREN AND THE LOVE OF FAMILY AND FRIENDS. (or, FOR THE GIFT OF SELF-CONFIDENCE AND THE SUPPORT OF FAMILY AND FRIENDS) THROUGH MY LIFE UNTIL NOW. AS A TOKEN OF MY GRATITUDE FOR WHAT HAS BEEN GIVEN TO ME I WISH TO BLESS AND CONSECRATE THESE COINS, ROUND AND SILVER LIKE THE MOON, AND GIVE THEM TO THOSE LESS FORTUNATE THAN MYSELF.

Pour the silver out on to the plate, covering the silver Crescent.

LIKE A SILVER TIDE, GOVERNED BY THE MOON'S POWER I GIVE THIS COIN TO BE USED FOR GOOD. I AM NOT HUNGRY, I AM NOT COLD, I AM NOT SICK UNTO DEATH. I AM NOT ALONE AND FRIENDLESS. I HAVE CLOTHES TO WEAR AND A HOME TO LIVE IN, I HAVE BEEN BLESSED MORE THAN I DESERVE. MOON MOTHER I OFFER THIS FOR YOUR BLESSING. (lift up plate) SHED THY SILVER LIGHT UPON IT THAT IT MAY DO GOOD.

I OFFER IT TO THE EAST . . . I OFFER IT TO THE SOUTH . . . I OFFER IT TO THE WEST . . . I OFFER IT TO THE NORTH . . . I CLEANSE IT WITH SALT AND WATER, I PASS IT THROUGH THE FLAME OF FIRE, I BREATHE UPON IT THE BREATH OF LIFE. I INVOKE MY CRONE POWER TO ENTER INTO ME AND FLOW THROUGH AND INTO THIS COIN FOR ITS BLESSING.

Place hand over plate and then puts it on altar.

I GIVE THANKS FOR ALL THAT I HAVE HAD, I GIVE THANKS FOR WHAT I HAVE AT THIS MOMENT, I ASK FOR GOOD FORTUNE TO ATTEND ME AND MY FAMILY INTO THE FUTURE.

FOR MY LIFE I GIVE THANKS, AND FOR MY MIND THAT IT IS CLEAR AND WITHOUT BLEMISH, AND FOR ALL MY DAYS TO COME BE THEY LONG OR SHORT I GIVE THANKS TO THE GREAT MOTHER THROUGH HER SYMBOL OF THE MOON. SO MOTE IT BE.

Re-trace the nine circles, going the opposite way and winding up the power. Then put out the lights. Place the coins in a clean cloth, rinse off the salted water and dry them in a towel. In the morning take them to a charity, or put them in a collecting box, or use them to buy a box of groceries for an elderly person living alone or in reduced circumstances.

Moon Party

The Japanese hold Moon-viewing parties and often build quite elaborate platforms on which to seat their guests. Sometimes they have special windows built into their houses in a particular direction so that they can watch the full moon as it rises over the sea, or over the garden where trees have been planted to frame her beauty.

Few people in the Western world even bother to look at the moon let alone spend a whole evening admiring it. To watch it rise over the gently rounded hills of England or over the Welsh mountains, the sea off the Norfolk coast, Glastonbury Tor, or the Malvern Hills is an unforgettable sight.

We have picnics in the Sunlight, so we can also have picnics in the Moonlight. A summer's evening under a full moon is an unusual but marvellous setting for a party. If you live near the sea and can get permission from the authorities to build a fire on the beach you will certainly have a night to remember. If the sea is too far away then look for a site where you can build a fire, but remember you will have to obtain permission from somewhere. It takes very little for a fire to get out of hand.

A party of about ten is the maximum, more than that and you will have to spend too much time arranging things. Try to find a place with an uninterrupted view of the moonrise, provide blankets on which to sit, and light refreshment. Wine, both white and red, open sandwiches or fresh bread rolls, a variety of cut meats and cheeses and perhaps fresh fruit is more than enough.

If people double up in cars it means only one person in each car has to keep to non-alcoholic drink. An alternative is to hire a mini-van and all come together with just one driver.

Ask just two or three people to bring a piece concerning the Moon to read out, one at the beginning, one while they are eating, and one to wind up the evening. Alternatively, write a pathworking which can be done either before or to conclude the evening. A cassette player with some appropriate and carefully chosen music played softly adds to the enjoyment. One of my most enduring memories is of sitting with some thirty people on the slopes of the Malvern Hills under a moon in a clear sky singing the old traditional songs of the Craft. Then, as the moon began to dip, walking back slowly to the centre, silent and full of peace.

It may not sound like much, but until you have tried it, you cannot know what such an experience can do for you. Lying on your back on fresh summer grass and looking at the Moon caught in the branches of a tree, like a silver fish in a net, can do more for you than some traditional rituals.

Remember that during your Crone years there are many opportunities to teach and train the younger women in the arts that you have learned over the years. Now is the time to pass on all the experience, information and expertise that you have acquired during the past years. Yours is now the position of honour and privilege, you are honour bound to pass on your knowledge.

The Vigil

Illness can strike at any time and sometimes it can mean that someone you love dearly may be taken from you. They may be in hospital, or at home, but it will mean long nights of watching and cat napping and days of anxiously waiting for the doctor. As we are born our length of days is born with us, there is nothing we can do about that. We have a given amount of time, not a second more nor less. When we marry, or even if we don't but simply live with someone, we do it with the hope that it will mean for the rest of our lives. Sometimes that comes true. In the small hours of the night hopes and dreams can sometimes get a little lost.

Vigils are held for different reasons – in ancient days a knight held a vigil on the eve of being dubbed as a knight. He placed his armour on the altar and leaned his sword against it, then knelt before it and prayed and meditated throughout the night. Sometimes a man or a woman preparing for ordination will opt to hold a vigil the night before in the church. When someone of note dies, a member of the royal family or a landowner, the body is laid in state and guarded by four people through the night. They are changed every so often to allow as many as possible to render this last service. A vigil can be held as a protest against something, or as part of a pilgrimage. But mostly we know a vigil as a nerve-racking watch over a loved one who is desperately ill. In the old days friends and neighbours would often take it in turns to watch over the sick to share some of the burden. Such caring is not often found in these modern times.

As a Crone, as one who has passed through many phases of the great work of the mysteries, you have inner strengths and powers which are not part of other people's characters. If such a task comes to you, you have more knowledge of how to cope than they would have. If you have to take your vigil in hospital, make sure you know where the chapel is. Almost every hospital will have one. Alternate your watch between the bedside and the chapel. This serves two purposes. One is that it will keep you awake in moving between them, the other is that it will enable you to concentrate your mind as you move from one atmosphere to the other.

In occult work of a long and tedious nature it is always best to break it up into smaller units of time. This helps you to pace yourself physically, mentally and spiritually. If you like, you can break this into three rather than two sessions, one in the chapel, one at the bedside, and one resting with instructions given to the night nurse to wake you at a given time, or a small and discreet travel alarm will do the same thing. A session should be long enough to make you feel you have accomplished something, not so long that you become even more fatigued. Twenty to thirty minutes for each one is about right. This will allow you to pray, to watch and to catch a sustaining cat nap without being out of touch for too long at any one time. Work it this way. Chapel, bed-watch, nap, bed-watch, chapel, bed-watch, and so on. This gives you twice as much bed-watch time as the others but still allows you time to rest and pray.

What we are most concerned with here is your time in the chapel. While on bed-watch you will want to hold a hand, talk gently and encouragingly to the patient. When you rest, do just that, don't allow yourself to lie there and think. Use your training to relax, breathe deeply and slide into sleep. You will be of more use if you are not incoherent with lack of sleep.

In the chapel it is another matter. You can use the time in one of two ways. Remember you do not have to explain the situation to the Inner Levels, they are fully aware of it. Neither is it possible to bargain, though the uninformed will always try. You *cannot* bargain for life, the Cosmic Law does not work that way. What you can do, if you have the strength is to *accept*. Kneel and open your heart and accept what is ordained to happen.

You do not have to struggle to find words either, simply kneel and concentrate your mind on the great archangelic presences that are always near at such times. If you are not of a Christian persuasion then call on your own God(dess) or God-forms. A place of worship is built for human beings to contact that which is greater than themselves. *We* are the ones who give it special names; on the higher levels there are no names as such, only forces of Love, Wisdom and Understanding. At such a level all becomes The One. Allow yourself to be comforted rather than seeking reassurance. What will happen will be for the best in all ways. Don't fumble for words – you will be too tired and too upset to make them into coherent sentences, just sit or kneel and *be with God(dess)*. Fill yourself up with strength, let it soak into you and take it back with you to the bedside.

If you feel you *must* speak words or pray, let them be simple and direct. Ask for strength to take back to your loved one. Ask for strength for yourself that you may not fail in your strength. Ask for understanding and wisdom. Do not make offers in return. Do a pathworking in your mind, it helps you to formulate what you need. Nothing elaborate, you might for instance simply sit at the side of Mary, or Jesus or Anubis or the Moon Mother, just quietly sit with them and allow them to heal you.

Imagine yourself sitting in the chapel with sunlight coming through the windows. The door opens and the person you are holding the vigil for comes in and stands beside you. You get up and, holding hands, walk out of the door into a hot dusty little town of mud-brick houses with flat roofs and lean-tos offering a little shade from the sun.

You walk together down the street, dressed as all the others are dressed in loose cotton robes and a light wooden shawl around your shoulders and head. You come to a small carpenter's shop with wooden cattle yokes and primitive ploughs outside. Inside it is cool and the young man smoothing a wooden stave looks up and smiles. He comes forward and offers you both some water then sits beside you, not talking, just sitting and looking. Then he takes the hand of your loved one and holds it, then he takes yours as well and you feel a warm strength pouring into you. After a while the man gets up and goes back to his work. You get up and leave, walking back to the place where you began, a ruined house no longer lived in. You enter its doorway and find yourself back in the chapel. Your loved one returns to the hospital bed and you wait a little while before leaving.

You can do the same kind of working but with Imhotep, or Isis, or Mary, Apollo or Aesculapius. Alternatively you can pathwork to a time when you were both together and in perfect health. Relive a special day or event.

What you must not do is sit and cry away your own strength.

Crone Right – The Second Road

As the Crone you have more powers of concentration than most, your years of training will have seen to that. You will of course have tried to channel healing into your loved one. You may have succeeded and brought them back to health. In that case on no account forget to give thanks for this grace.

You must be prepared, however, to let go if you must. If it becomes apparent that the silver cord will soon be cut, then, but not until then, you may exercise Crone Right to call the Angel of Death. The Old Wise Woman is she who stands at the door of life and death. She is both the Midwife and the

Layer-Out. The newborn and the dead both pass through her hands. If the one who is passing is an initiate then they may wish for things to be done according to the way of their Lodge. You will find all the information you need on the differing ceremonies, etc in *The New Book of the Dead* (Aquarian 1992).

If the passing takes place at home then you will need to set up the circle in the room itself. This need not be conspicuous, the actual circle itself can be set while they are asleep. In fact. it is a good idea to set up a circle around a sick bed at any time since it keeps at bay those entities that are drawn by sickness and ill health and which prey on fears and sleeplessness and dark dreams. It is done according to whatever tradition you wish. The Qabalistic, the Hermetic, the Rose Cross are especially good since its enclosing is very secure. You can, if you wish, simply imagine three circles of light encompassing the whole room.

Set up a small table to one side with a white cloth, a chalice with a small amount of wine, a piece of bread or a wafer, oil, salt and water already blessed, and four candles, one for each of the quarter archangels, or the elemental kings of the quarters or Godforms if you prefer to work with them. Your Crone Right is valid right through tradition since the right of the Wise Woman to act both as a Midwife and as a Death-Wife goes beyond mere traditions set up by humans.

See that the patient is washed and put into clean clothes and clean bed linen. The bathing and clean clothing also applies to you. Work when the patient is asleep as far as is possible in order not to disturb or upset them.

Begin the ritual as follows:

Sprinkle the patient very lightly with salt and water.

IN THE NAME OF .... I CLEANSE THEE WITH THE SALT OF THE EARTH AND THE WATERS OF THE MOON. (put the tiniest piece of bread or wafer between their lips)

IN THE NAME OF .... I OFFER YOU BREAD FOR YOUR JOURNEY BEYOND THE SUNSET. (with your finger dipped in the wine, place a drop on their lips)

IN THE NAME OF .... I GIVE YOU WINE FOR YOUR JOURNEY TO THE PLACE OF PEACE AND REGENERATION. (anoint forehead, breast, hands and the soles of the feet with oil)

IN THE NAME OF .... I ANOINT YOU IN PREPARATION FOR YOUR JOURNEY BEYOND MORTAL REACH. (light each candle with a separate invocation)

1st Candle: I, ..., INVOKE THEE RAPHAEL, REGENT OF THE ELEMENT OF AIR THAT BY YOUR AID .... MAY BE TRANSPORTED THROUGH YOUR ELEMENT TO A PLACE OF REST AND PEACE. BY THE AUTHORITY OF CRONE RIGHT I SUMMON YOU TO THIS PLACE. LET THIS BE MADE KNOWN TO YOU. *2nd Candle*: I, ..., INVOKE THEE MICHAEL, REGENT OF THE ELEMENT OF FIRE, THAT BY YOUR AID .... MAY PASS THROUGH YOUR ELEMENT THUS BURNING AWAY THE DROSS OF THE PHYSICAL AND GOING ON TO A PLACE OF SILENCE AND HEALING. BY THE AUTHORITY OF CRONE RIGHT I SUMMON YOU TO THIS PLACE. LET THIS BE MADE KNOW TO YOU.

3rd Candle: I, ..., INVOKE THEE GABRIEL, REGENT OF THE ELEMENT OF WATER, THAT BY YOUR AID .... MAY PASS THROUGH YOUR ELEMENT THUS WASHING AWAY THE LAST REMNANT OF PHYSICAL LIFE AND COMING FRESH AND CLEAN TO A PLACE OF LAUGHTER AND SWEET DREAMS. BY THE AUTHORITY OF CRONE RIGHT I SUMMON YOU TO THIS PLACE. LET THIS BE MADE KNOWN TO YOU.

4th Candle: I, ..., INVOKE THEE URIEL, REGENT OF THE ELEMENT OF EARTH, THAT BY YOUR AID .... MAY LEAVE YOUR ELEMENT BEHIND FOR THIS INCARNATION AND PASS BEYOND IT TO A PLACE OF LOVE, BEAUTY AND WISDOM. BY THE AUTHORITY OF CRONE RIGHT I SUMMON YOU TO THIS PLACE. LET THIS BE MADE KNOWN TO YOU.

(go to stand at the foot of the bed and cup your hands together and bow your head).

GREAT AND HOLY ONE, WHOSE WINGS ARE LIKE THE SHADES OF NIGHT DRAWN NEAR TO THIS PLACE, SPREAD THY HEALING PEACE OVER THIS ROOM AND THIS MAN/WOMAN. FILL THE MIND WITH A DREAM OF LOVE, FILL THE HEART WITH PEACE AND TRUST, FILL THE SOUL WITH FAITH AND HOPE. I SUMMON THEE BY CRONE RIGHT, TO ATTEND .... AND CARRY THE SOUL GENTLY THROUGH THE GATES OF TRANS-

MUTATION AND INTO THE LIGHT. I OPEN THE DOOR TO THEE SABLE-WINGED LORD OF THE PASSING, I HAVE CLEANSED AND HALLOWED, I HAVE GIVEN FOOD AND DRINK FOR THE JOURNEY, I HAVE ANOINTED WITH OIL AND MADE HOLY THE PHYSICAL BODY OF .... BY CRONE RIGHT I CALL THEE, ATTEND THY DUTIES, WHILE I SING THE DEATH SONG.

The Death Song is a very ancient tradition whereby one sings or chants the story of one's life, condensing it but touching on the most important events. It need not be sung by the one leaving, but can, as in this instance, be chanted by the Crone. For an example see *The New Book of the Dead* page 150, and below.

I, ..., leapt into life in a place of hills and valleys.
Filled with song and the sound of laughter was my childhood.
I ran with my brothers over the high cwms and deep vales,
Catching dreams and making them into kites. I grew away from
    the hills and left them behind,
but my heart stood on the hills and called to me.
I was a man without a heart.
Into my life came a companion, sweet-faced and gentle.
A golden ring was my pledge to her and hers to me.
In laughter and in tears we made our way through life together.
A girl child, then a son, and another, they filled us with wonder
    and gave us a dream for the future.
My heart still called to me from the hills and
we travelled the road back at last.
Honest work, but no great wealth, small joys and some sorrows
fell upon us like rain through the years.
I have made no great way in the world, I am a man of the
    people
I have striven to be good, I have been at fault,
but I have loved and been loved in return.
I have seen my children grow and their children gather about
    me.
I have taught them the old tongue and the old songs.
Now I must leave my laughing girl and the high Hills
for another place unknown and unseen.
Take my hand in yours and hold it tightly
pass my hand into the hand of that which comes for me.
One last song, one last look at my Hills,
let me pass and leave only my footstep upon the grass.

The song touches lightly, making just a faint echo of the life story. When this has been chanted make your farewells and await the coming of the most gentle and most beautiful of all Inner Level Beings.

PART 5
WINTER
Hibernation

13

THE GOLDEN YEARS

This time of our lives can be both sweet and poignant. We can think of so many things that we meant to do and somehow or other never quite managed to get around to doing. We begin to think about the time we have wasted and what we could do with that time now. We must realise that there are some things for which it is too late, but a lot of things we can still get done, things to enjoy.

In our modern world many seventy-year-olds are still highly active and alert – there is no reason to think that you are 'over the hill' at this age. But you will not be able to rush around as you once did. Where you used to go visiting, now people will have to get used to visiting you instead.

The latter years of Cronehood, if you have been active in the Mysteries during your life, can be very rewarding, as many people come seeking you for training and for advice. You have time now to refine the teaching you have given to those destined to follow you. Time also to point out those who in your opinion show promise.

Your memories are valuable, get someone to take them down so that there will be no doubt as to what you meant, what you said, how you felt about certain things, or even people. You may like to begin your memoirs yourself, if not then get someone you can trust to do it. Anyone who has lived a fairly long and full life has important information to pass on. If this is not done then old traditions and pieces of important information disappear for ever.

Now is also the time to give away things that have been precious to you, making sure that they go where they will be appreciated and continue to be used. You will also have the fun of seeing how much the gifts are appreciated as coming from you.

Nobody is thinking in terms of death, but when you reach this age you should have made certain that everything is in order and nothing you want done has been left unsaid. Planning one's funeral is, after all, no more than planning any other kind of celebration. It is time also to heal old hurts and make sure that as far as is possible you will leave no rancour behind.

BUT, go on enjoying yourself, go on working with magic and the mysteries in all forms. You may not be able to travel as much or as far, but do a little and keep your mind active. Gather the young people around you and you will find you still have things to say that are relevant.

In Japan they have people who are declared to be National Treasures, people who have been special in some way that makes the whole country proud of them. Being needed and being useful are things that older people need very much. But you also need time to yourself for you still have things to seek out, things to resolve and get clear in your own head.

You may find as you pass your seventies and head into your eighties that you will need to leave your home and many of your familiar things. It may be that you need special care, or that you are no longer able completely to look after yourself. If you come from a long-lived family you can look forward to the high eighties and even nineties, a hundred is not inconceivable these days. It will be a wrench to leave a home in which you have lived for a good part of your life. There will be tears when things must be sold or given away, or even thrown out. Remember your training, they are just 'things' – things to which we have become unduly attached – it is right that we should have a chance to disentangle ourselves from them before they become an intolerable burden.

To give up your precious independence and perhaps, if it is something you treasure, the pleasure of silence, and enter a place where it is all hustle and bustle and determined cheerfulness, is painful. If you have been trained to it you still can have the inner silence, there is still your own 'inner kingdom' where you are no longer old but young and agile. By mastering the art of the inner kingdom now, you will lay down treasures for your old age.

There may be something you are holding on to see or to accomplish, a great grandchild being christened, or even married. Something you have striven for all your life may come to fruition. By all means seek to achieve this, but then let go and claim your Crone Right and send out the call loud and clear as in the old days. Summon your gentle friend, give yourself up to his strength and go with the dawn light.

If I may speak to the younger ones who, hopefully, will be reading this: if you have someone much older, remember that they can get lonely and feel forgotten. Remember also that they still have a need to feel useful and a fount of information to give to those who will ask. Younger people are often selfish without meaning to be, it is only when it is almost too late that we think that we should have spent more time with those we love. 'If only . . .' are the saddest words of all.

This is a sunset time, usually the most beautiful time of the day, though others prefer the dawn. I know that I shall remember sunsets most of all. I shall remember an April evening on a deserted Jersey beach with the sun descending and the moon already visible, holding the evening star in her curve, the sky colours of palest turquoise, rose and gold. That was the moment when I finally came to terms with the fact that I had taken on the job of following in the footsteps of my teacher; the moment when I accepted an inner level contact as my lifelong companion. Yes, for me it will always be the setting sun rather than its rising. Not surprising really when that contact is the Guider of Souls himself.

It seems a long time, Daughter of Eve, since we began this journey through your life. You have passed through many Rites of Passage and experienced many things. You have many memories to entertain you in the last days – your first day at school: can you remember the colour of the new pencil box your mother bought you? The excitement when you reached the first double-figure birthday, and the even greater excitement when you became a real teenager; the embarrassment when your first flowing appeared and the sweetness of your first kiss . . . whatever did happen to him?

Your engagement party when you nearly lost your new ring down the sink because it was a size too large and the wedding day when he stepped on your veil and wrecked your hairdo? Honeymoon and new home, your first car, your very own home, and then the new baby and having to sell the car to buy the nursery furniture. So many joys and tears in one year.

Remember the time when you thought your marriage was going to break up and you packed his bags and left them in the hall? And do you remember making up in the garden shed where he had spent the night with the temperature below freezing?! Oh yes, and the panic at your own daughter's wedding and wondering how your own mother could have coped with all this . . . several times. It's been a marvellous life, and there is a lot of it yet to be lived. Put this book down and go out and buy a new dress. There are a few Rites to end this book, but until the very last one, keep looking for something new to learn, to experience. Keep your child's heart, Daughter of Eve, try to laugh every day if you can – laughter is a wonderful medicine.

14

THE RITUALS

The Garden of Memories

Not all rituals are done around an altar, in a Lodge or in a Woodland Circle. Some are images and symbols put together in a pattern that will persist. This is such a one. It is the building of a pattern that portrays a lifetime.

The gift of memory is a very precious thing and the more we can do to help us remember things the better our life will be. There is nothing quite like a garden for holding memories, and a memory garden can bring you hours of happiness throughout your life.

When you move into your first home, plant a tree at the front of the house to act as a welcome to all the people who will come to your door in the years to come. Choose it carefully so that it will be a showpiece. Type out a short piece explaining what the tree is, the event it symbolises, the date and perhaps a short verse. Add a photograph and put it in an album. Add photos of the tree as it grows. But this is not the end. Make every event in your life the reason to plant a living memory, a shrub, another tree, a climbing rose over an archway. The album then becomes the record of a living ritual of your life throughout the years. If you choose wisely they will grow and give beauty and character to the whole garden.

When something is done with intent, and is repeated at intervals, we call it a ritual. We make a ritual out of measuring our children each birthday; out of a special dinner on an anniversary. They are nothing like a ritual as we, trained in the work of the mysteries, understand the word. Nevertheless, such a deliberate planting of living symbols of events in our lives makes of a simple garden a holy place, as holy as any temple or lodge.

Choosing the plant becomes something to which we can look forward. One part of the garden becomes the 'anniversary' place, where every tree, shrub and plant is an on-going reminder of your years together. It may be purely a rose garden with a different kind each year. A special, expensive and very new one on the special dates, for instance the Silver, Pearl and Ruby anniversaries. Planted on the evening before it can be part of the ritual to lead your mother or wife out into the garden early the next morning to view the new arrival. Later, when perhaps your partner leaves you behind, the children and grandchildren can take on the task.

A new baby means a new sapling to plant, an engagement or a wedding in the family might mean the planting of twin trees. The album will grow with the garden, and in the future it will be something to show to the younger ones: 'This is *your* tree, the one we planted when you were born. And this one is your mother's tree.'

Each planting might be done with a simple ritual. Once the place is decided upon the hole is dug ready to receive the new arrival. Take a few grains of incense to lay at the bottom, a few grains of salt, a silver coin or a little box containing a memento of the day to act as a time capsule. Bless the little plant in the name of Serapis, he who is sometimes called 'The Gardener of God'. Call upon the nature devas to welcome it and make sure of its survival. Plant it and water it well with water from a holy well, or at least water that has been blessed.

If you have no garden but would still like to do something of this kind, there is nothing to prevent you from purchasing a sapling and going out into the country to plant it in a wood. Or you can give money to a group such as The Men of the Trees and they will see that a tree is planted in your name. Many conservation groups have a similar scheme. You will leave the world a lot richer for your caring and your love.

The Giving

We all collect things, too many things, and there is a time when we get an urge to give things away. Often the things themselves suggest it, it is made clear to us in one way or another that it no longer belongs to us, but to someone else. So why not make the idea of giving into a special ritual, where you can gather the people you love together and pass on your treasures. It is also an excuse for a feast and a get together.

You will need an altar with the usual white cloth, a Chalice of wine to share, a centre light (perhaps a special candle might be made for you – Fantasy Candles[1] can make special ones for any occasion in special colours and with a choice of perfumes), some salt and water and a thurible of light incense. On another table behind you, put all the things you wish to give away, clearly labelled and covered with a white cloth. Gather everyone into a circle and seat them around the room. Ask one of them to perform the Rose Cross opening. Sprinkle around the altar with blessed salt and water, circle with the thurible and begin with a short invocation.

IN THE NAME OF THAT ONE CREATOR OF ALL THINGS, THAT POINT WHERE ALL TRADITIONS, FAITHS, AND GODS MEET, I WELCOME YOU ALL HERE. I INVOKE UPON THIS GATHERING THE BLESSING OF LIGHT. I OFFER THANKS FROM THE DEPTHS OF MY HEART FOR ALL THAT I HAVE RECEIVED IN MY LIFE AND FOR THE LOVE OF THOSE I SEE AROUND ME TONIGHT.

I AM MINDFUL OF THE FACT THAT WE CAN TAKE NOTHING OUT OF THIS WORLD AND I THINK IT WOULD BE A GOOD THING TO PASS ON TO YOU CERTAIN THINGS THAT I HAVE LOVED AND TREASURED. I HOPE THAT YOU WILL LOVE THEM AS I HAVE DONE, AND USE THEM AND PERHAPS, ONE DAY, PASS THEM ON AGAIN.

I HAVE THOUGHT LONG AND HARD ABOUT WHAT SHOULD GO TO WHOM, I HOPE I HAVE MADE THE RIGHT CHOICES. IF I HAVE NOT, AND YOU FEEL THAT WHAT I GIVE TO YOU SHOULD GO TO SOMEONE ELSE, PLEASE SAY SO AFTER I HAVE FINISHED AND IF THAT PERSON AGREES YOU MAY EXCHANGE IT WITH MY BLESSING.

Now call each one to the altar and give them their gift. Explain in a few words why you want them to have it, perhaps a little of its history. (You can write this out and put it in an envelope to go with the object if you wish.) Do not wrap the gift – let them see it and enjoy it right away – besides, a lot of paper means the life of a tree. Before they leave the altar ask them to share a sip of wine with you (*just* a sip on your part or you will end up on the floor!).

It is no good giving away the things you don't want or need. Real giving has to hurt a little. The things you are giving now are things you would really like to keep a little longer. Things which in your heart you know you seldom or never wear (jewellery), or have had in a cupboard because there is nowhere with enough space to display it (silver). Or it may need to find an owner who will treasure it because it will otherwise get thrown out or sold at a jumble sale later (books and ornaments).

When all has been given away, close with a short invocation to your favourite Godform and a blessing on your family and friends. Then invite them to help you close and clear things away and join you in a feast.

The Golden Sphere

This is more in the nature of a pathworking and is meant to be a comfort to you if you ever have to leave your home and enter sheltered housing, or find yourself having to go into a home of any kind. It needs to be built as a precaution against these things. You really need to build it a little bit at a time and get it really right before going on to the next part.

Build up before you a very large golden sphere. It is opaque and seems to be made of something similar to cracked glass. Spend some time on this, get it just right and view it from all angles. Take at least a week until you can visualise it with very little effort.

During the next week search for the door. It is in there somewhere, but carefully hidden. However, once you have found it you will always be able to find it. Now you have found it you need to know how to open it, this will take you on average the rest of the week.

The next phase is entering the sphere. Build it up, find the door, open it and look inside. Remember it is very big. When you step inside you find that it is even bigger. In fact you cannot see where it ends or how high it is. There appears to be a bright sun overhead, in fact you get the oddest feeling that once inside the sphere, you are in another universe, or at the very least another dimension of this one. You are exactly right. Inside this sphere you will build the world you know, but to your own specifications.

The first week you will need to build your immediate environment, the area in which you now live. Houses, shops, markets, schools and churches – everything. Do a little each day and when you are out, observe minutely each detail. Pay particular attention to your own house and build it as you would like it to be, changing the decorations, size, etc. From then on you need to build little by little all the places you know well from the past and from the present. You might like to separate the past from the present by a river and one bridge that crosses over into the long ago.

There may be some places of which you are particularly fond, a holiday place, for instance – build it into the sphere exactly as you remember it. The sphere is infinite, it can take as much as you want to put into it. It has no limit. Now you can begin to people it with images of friends and family, again past and present. You will find that the sphere has a day and a night and also seasons of the year and even different climates. You can train yourself to do anything you enjoy doing in the physical world – eating, swimming, gardening, cooking, playing golf, etc. This is an inner world for you to enjoy. If you have to go into hospital you will find it useful. You can rest quietly and still be somewhere else doing what you want to do. If you enjoy travel then you can travel within the sphere.

If you ever have to leave a place you love, it will still be here for you. So can the people you love. Friends with whom you may have lost touch can be found here. Old pets can be found again, your youth can be explored again and perhaps different avenues in life explored and experienced without alarm because you can always go back to the point at which you deviated.

One small point, however. Never let yourself get so attached to this work that you do not wish to leave. Discipline yourself to short visits. The danger is that you can get glamoured by the sphere and part company with reality.

When someone is near to the end of life, or if they are suffering pain, then it can be of great value and the stay can be made gradually longer until the physical and the subtle blend into one and the soul slips gently away.

The White Door

We must all say goodbye one day. It is painful and we all fight against it in our own way. It is harder for those left behind than for those that leave.

It is best if the soul realises right away that there is no way back. If you can make yourself go forward and resist the temptation to look back it will be much easier in the long run. Remember how Orpheus looked back and lost his Eurydice? How Lot's wife looked back and was turned into salt? Looking back at such times does no good at all and only makes the parting much more painful than it needs to be.

Again, this is more a pathworking than a ritual. Build in your mind a winding path that wanders over fields and hills bright with heather. In the distance you can see a range of mountains with snow-capped peaks. Behind you there is only a white mist, thick and impenetrable. Follow the path along until it becomes a dirt track, and then a lane with hedges on either side. Finally, on one side you see a high wall of dressed stone. Follow this along for a while until you come to a white door set into the wall. There is a handle but no lock. There is no way you can enter unless it is opened from the inside.

Turn around and begin to make your way back. As you go you see that over the high wall there must be a garden of some kind, for roses climb over the wall and honeysuckle tendrils hang over it. Off to your left you can see a fairly high hill with a crown of trees on top. If you climb up you might be able to see over the wall.

You set off over a field to the foot of the hill and begin to clamber up its steep slopes. It gets harder as you near the top and you have to stop several times to get your breath. When you do reach it, however, you find you can see right over the wall. There is a semi-wild garden and an orchard to one side. You can see a glimpse of woodland that seems to lead away to the right and on to the mountains. Just visible among the trees is a cottage with a thatched roof and a blaze of colourful flowers all around it. A plume of smoke rises from the chimney and from far off you can hear someone singing. Below the cottage you can see either a broad river or maybe the sea – an estuary perhaps.

You climb back down the hill and retrace your steps the way you came, finally entering the mist and finding yourself where you started. The white door is the entry to the very last Rite of Passage. Hold its image in your mind as your life closes and it will appear before you. You will know it is time to go because it will stand open, inviting you to go through. Do not look back, it is kinder. There are people waiting for you at the cottage. Be blessed in your going, and in your eventual return.

Notes

1 Fantasy Candles,
  Glanrhyd,
  Clydogau,
  Nr Lampeter,
  Dyfed SA4 8LJ

Epilogue

Daughter of Eve, I thank you for sharing this book with me.
Whether you are young or old, a follower of the Goddess or
devoted to another faith of the Light, I wish you well on your
journey through life. To those I have already met with and
who have become dear to me let me say to you that you have
enriched my life. To those I have still to meet, know that I
stand ready to welcome you into my life. Be Blessed.

Bibliography

Meditations for Children, Deborah Rozman, Celestial Arts Inc, 1976.

Story Telling and the Art of the Imagination, Nancy Mellon, Element, 1992.

First Steps in Ritual, Dolores Ashcroft-Nowicki, Aquarian, 1982/1990.

The Tree of Ecstasy, Dolores Ashcroft-Nowicki, Aquarian, 1991.

Highways of the Mind, Dolores Ashcroft-Nowicki, Aquarian, 1987.

The New Book of the Dead, Dolores Ashcroft-Nowicki, Aquarian, 1992.

The Wise Wound, Penelope Shuttle and Peter Redgrove, Gollancz, 1978/Paladin, 1986.

Children at Play, H. Britz-Crecelius, Floris, 1972.

Index